Tough Questions, Honest Answers

Tough Questions, Honest Answers

Faith and Religion for 21st-Century Explorers

Cameron Harder

Fortress Press

Minneapolis

TOUGH QUESTIONS, HONEST ANSWERS

Faith and Religion for 21st-Century Explorers

Cover Image: Circular motion of stars around the Polar Star stock photo by
Vadven. iStock © 2016.

Cover Design: Lauren Williamson

Print ISBN: 978-1-5064-5384-2

Ebook ISBN: 978-1-5064-5385-9

Contents

Preface

Welcome! I hope you have packed your curiosity and capacity for careful reflection as we set out to explore. Beware, however! This book is not a Google map detailing with digital accuracy every nook and cranny of the questions we'll cover. It's more like a pirate's map roughly scrawled on the back of a page torn from a sailor's almanac, with an "X" to mark treasure in one corner and the warning, "here be dragons," in another.

Exploring, especially on the sort of rocky ground we'll cover, is best done with a companion or a group. While I'll tell you what I've been thinking, I want to provoke and intrigue you as much as inform. So, on some of the more difficult topics, you may benefit from having an open-minded conversation partner or group to help you sort out your own thoughts. It will also be more fun trying out the exercises at the end of each chapter with others.

A few things should be clarified before we begin:

1. This is neither a "tell all" nor a defense of religion, though I will share some of religion's gaffs and gifts. It is mainly an effort to frame some current hard questions about religion in twenty-first-century Western language and thought. It is a book that young parents,

for example, can turn to when they have been a bit turned off (or just not turned on) by religion, and they are wondering how to nurture their child's spirituality. Or, this book might be useful for older readers who have been involved with a religious community for a long time but want to rethink their faith in light of what they've learned about the world over the decades.

2. I use the term "religion" in the ordinary way we use it in the United States and Canada, where religion is distinguished from "worldly" or "secular" things and is lodged in discrete organizations with distinct structures and histories. This way of viewing religion, however, is a relatively recent development. For most of human history, and still in many cultures around the world, "religion" is not about *organizations*. It is simply an aspect of community life, a part of the glue that binds people together, a way of carrying the hopes and struggles of a community before the great Mysteries, and a mechanism for dealing with fear and stress.

3. I try to provide an interreligious context for the questions that are posed in this book, but my extensive training is in Christian theology and practice. I have tried to be accurate when I make reference to other traditions, but please accept my apologies if you discover a place where facts or interpretations are distorted.

4. This is not primarily an academic book. It touches on lots of issues. I won't try to exhaustively share the history or current thinking for each one. This book is largely the result of my own experience and reflection, so I have tried to reduce reference notes to a minimum. However, in a few places—the chapter on religion and child sexual abuse especially—I felt it was important to

give you direct access to the facts. Where possible, I have included web addresses for my sources in the bibliography so you can follow up on them if you like.

5. The term "honest answers" in the book title does not mean that there is a definitive answer to any of the large questions being posed. Instead, it is my effort to be *personally* honest with the questions, to push past the platitudes and propaganda that sometimes cloud my perspective on the work I've been doing for forty years. I'm an explorer too—looking for a clearer view of what religion could be, and should not be, for my children and grandchildren.

6. Finally, the questions themselves are not just my own. Some emerged from research that I did with people who were encountering religion for the first time. Others have been suggested by a group of folks who read and responded to my blogs about these topics over the last year or so. Some are active churchgoers, some aren't. And feedback from my editor—Beth Gaede—and her team has been invaluable. All have helped me stay honest and on track.

Above all, my gratitude goes out to my long-suffering wife, Dory, who thought that we would spend our retirement reading in the garden together but instead has found me closeted in a dark hole downstairs writing for hours every day. Now it's her turn!

1

Why Take on Tough Questions about Religion?

In the twenty-first century, faith faces a paradox. On one hand, life in our globalized world is so *complex* that many long for simplicity, a safe bubble where they can live with unquestioning confidence in their religious traditions. On the other hand, it is impossible to avoid the tumult of voices raising hard questions about religion. Those questions threaten to burst the bubble, disrupt our peace, even cut us off from our faith community. Yet they also bring potential for new insight and spiritual growth.

A bit of my own story might illustrate the tension. A few years ago I began to hear, firsthand, the stories of Indian residential school survivors in Canada. Some accounts were horrific: children forcibly separated from parents at very young ages; thousands dying from exposure and malnutrition because the schools were poorly funded, so young children were forced to work in brutal conditions to support them; six-year-olds beaten and humiliated for speaking their native languages; young children routinely sexually assaulted by older children and even a few teachers; forced conversion to Christianity; and so on. I was shocked by the intergenerational legacy of PTSD, addictions, and broken families that were left behind. And I learned that every Christian church in my country was complicit either of running a school (twelve denominations) or *ignoring* the damage the schools were doing (all the others).

At the time, I was a seminary professor. You can imagine my struggle. Should I be training leaders for organized religion when religion in Canada has been heavily implicated in violence against children and cultural genocide for the last 150 years?

I talked to a career counselor, telling her how deeply this discovery had shaken my view of the religious world in which I was immersed. She listened carefully but then said, "I'm sure there are many things that would shake up my life too if I was aware of them. But I can't manage that much chaos. If I'm going to survive, I just have to shut some things out, stay in my comfortable bubble."

Honestly, I was tempted. I saw the pain and shame that survivors felt as they told their stories. I felt the distress in my own gut as their stories shattered my image of who I was as a Canadian and a religious leader. But I encountered aboriginal survivors in my extended family; they couldn't be ignored. And I knew that healing for our nation wouldn't begin until that dark reality was faced.

But here is the dilemma. Not all indigenous survivors have the support they need to face their wounded history without crippling pain and shame. And not all settlers are able to face the economic, physical, or social violence in which their family may have participated. Sometimes, a bubble may be necessary, at least for a while.

Reasons for Not Looking Too Hard at Religious Traditions

"TMI" (too much information) is a popular online acronym. It's often used when folks find out more than they want to about cherished things. For example, children may groan, crying "TMI!" when they hear about their parents' love life. Even less do most of us want to know the painful or unsavory bits hidden in the closets of friends, role models, and valued institutions. Here are some good reasons why some readers may find this book "TMI" and not want to engage tough questions about faith and religion.

Ignorance can be adaptive

As my career counselor suggested, life isn't easy. Humans have always struggled to keep food on the table, clothes on the kids, and a roof over our heads. Over the millennia, our brains evolved very sensitive mechanisms to alert us to anything that might threaten our basic needs. Unfortunately, the world is a dangerous place. We could be paralyzed by fear if we truly knew how frail are things we most rely on—our bodies, our social networks, religious authorities, our systems of government and finance, the teachers and media that provide our understanding of the world. So, the courage to act requires some blindness to life's risks.

In other words, the hope that plunges us into life's great experiment has to be a bit *naïve*. For example, a young woman meets someone through an online dating site and sets up a face-to-face date. Will they like each other as much in person? What will they discover about each other that isn't on their online profiles (and that they may not want the other to know)? There's no way to be sure until they meet. Those who dare such intimate encounters do so because they are fortified with a strong dose of naïve hope. (Without it our species would be extinct!)

The same dynamic functions on a communal level. Working

with depressed rural communities, I discovered that it was often counterproductive to identify and analyze their problems in detail. It seemed to increase their shared sense of shame and hopelessness. So I began to use approaches that build courage and self-esteem: *Appreciative Inquiry* asks questions such as "What is *working* in your community right now?" "What do you value most about your community and why?" *Asset-mapping* asks, "What resources do you *already* have in this community that you are willing to share (gifts of personality, access to natural resources, personal items, time, skills, and the like) and how could they be imaginatively combined to strengthen your life together?" Being too aware of problems can paralyze communities. These hope-building processes help people get out of their common depression and give them energy to work on a better future for their town.[1]

Faith can work even as a "placebo"

When people believe that their problems no longer have a stranglehold on them, they are more likely to get better, *even if the treatment is an illusion.*

There are numerous studies verifying this phenomenon in medicine. Science journalist Claudia Willis mentions several in an article entitled, "Why Fake Operations Are a Good Thing."[2] She notes that in a British study, patients with a blocked artery who were given a fake stent operation showed as much improvement as patients who had a real one. Willis also describes a meta-analysis of seventy-nine studies for migraine prevention which found that sugar pills reduced headache frequency for 22 percent of patients, fake acupuncture helped 38 percent of patients, and sham surgery was a hit for a remarkable 58 percent.

Why does it help to believe something that isn't real? Perhaps because those who believe they are getting better are more likely to talk about it to friends and loved ones. Those folks generally offer support (which pumps serotonin and dopamine into the brain) and sometimes helpful advice as well. The patient's health may improve because they are better connected and have new energy and strategies to address their illness.

For some people, faith operates in a similar way. Because they believe faith will help them, it *does*. They face crises with less anxiety, join with other believers in supporting each other, and derive meaning for their lives from their faith. Even if faith is an illusion, piercing the illusion might not be helpful.

"Virtual" reality is the only kind available

None of us actually knows—or could handle if we did—"the truth, the whole truth, and nothing but the truth" about anything (though that's what most Western nations require of their court witnesses!). So we create a reality for ourselves that's more manageable.

I had a disturbing experience of this one late fall night as I was driving through a relatively unpopulated part of the prairies. There was no moon, no snow, no natural light. The Milky Way was brilliant—a thick band of stardust across the sky. The northern lights were dancing in their seductive green and burgundy dresses. The view was so compelling I had to stop the car (I was driving erratically with my nose up to the windshield!). I got out and lay down in a field on my back to get the full effect. Suddenly something happened that frightened me deeply: my awareness shifted. The air was so clear it seemed the atmosphere disappeared, and the earth flipped. I was staring *down* into space, as if a vast black abyss of stars and kaleidoscopic color had opened beneath me and I was about to fall in. Without thinking I grabbed the ground with both hands, hanging on for dear life. For just a moment, I realized what a tiny mote I am in this enormous universe and how very fragile I am. If it wasn't for the earth's secure embrace, I knew I would not last a second in that frigid expanse.

For a moment, I saw things as they really are. Experiences like those are disturbing, enchanting, a "wonder-full" terror. But one can't *live* in them. An indigenous elder once told me, "Don't stare at the northern lights too long—they'll steal your soul."

Truth is, we need a "skin" over reality to make the world habitable. So our minds construct a "virtual reality" that allows us to go about our business in relative comfort:

- Northerners fret about cold weather unaware that we stand on a great ball of molten lava, protected from its blistering heat by a skin thinner, proportionately, than that of an apple.

- We rest at night oblivious to the fact that our bodies are hurtling through space in complicated spirals at astonishing speeds, rotating with the earth at about 1000 mph, revolving around the sun at about 67,000 mph, revolving with our sun around the center of our Milky Way galaxy at about 483,000 mph, and moving with our galaxy in relation to the cosmic background radiation at 1.3 million mph.[3]

- Our physical senses tell us that we are substantial beings, surrounded by solid stuff that we can eat, see, smell, hear, and manipulate. But physicists tell us that we and all other material things are composed almost entirely of energy fields and vortices. The tiny bits of atomic matter that anchor those energies are so dense that a pure spoonful, for example, from a collapsed neutron star, would have a mass equivalent to hundreds of millions of tons on earth. We are (as our mothers suspected when we were teens) mostly empty space.

There are many other examples of the way in which we place a skin over reality to make it livable. We hide the plumbing, wiring, and studs of our home's infrastructure behind drywall. We keep most of our random thoughts of judgment, irritation, and admiration inside our heads where family and coworkers can't see them. On our computers, we install "graphical user interfaces" (GUIs) in the form of various apps so that we don't have to deal with the complex tangle of circuits and machine code that make up computer reality. Playing *Super Mario Odyssey* on our laptop, we don't seem disturbed that there are not actually tiny Italian plumbers running around inside. In fact, it is much easier to get something done with a computer if we don't look too closely at its electronic mysteries.

As I will explore in more detail later, religions are virtual constructs too. The Broadway play, *The Book of Mormon*, has many faults (especially in its portrayal of Africans), but one thing it does get right in my opinion is its insistence that faith can only be expressed in metaphor. And the power of metaphors is dependent on context. In one setting, particular metaphors may provide healing, reconciliation, or hope, while the same images and stories may provoke fear or justify abuse in another setting.

In the musical, Elder Cunningham finds that traditional Book of Mormon images aren't connecting with the Ugandan villagers. So he eventually creates "The Book of Arnold"—a comic collection of images from the *Lord of the Rings* and *Star Wars*—which he uses to help the villagers resist the practice of female circumcision and the rape of infants as well as free themselves from the tyranny of the local warlord.

I'm not singling out Mormonism. Every religion has fantastical elements. Judaism has Balaam's talking donkey, a burning-but-never-consumed bush, and Elisha's bottomless cups of oil and flour. Christianity has bread turning into flesh, water into wine, corpses walking out of their tombs. Hindu descriptions of demigods and chimeric creatures are particularly implausible: Rompo has the head of a hare, human ears, a badger's arms, a bear's legs on a skeleton body; Ganesh has a human body with four arms and the head of an elephant.

In many ways, religions serve as cultural GUIs (perhaps "*God*-user-interfaces" instead of graphical user interfaces?). They provide vivid rites and images that help satisfy the human need to make meaning out of a very complex and mysterious universe precisely *because they are mythical and metaphorical* in character. And they provide simple life hacks to assist personal and communal growth:

- "Do unto others as you would have them do unto you" and "Love the Lord with all your heart, mind and strength and your neighbor as yourself," Jesus said.

- "Strive to let go of all attachments," advised the Buddha.

- "Honor your father and mother and your own days will be lengthened," Moses commanded.

- "The greatest of wealth is the richness of the soul," the prophet Muhammad taught.

Our complex world can be overwhelming, and such simplifications at least give us a starting point for action.

Disenchantment is painful

When the movie *Avatar* came out at Christmas 2009, many viewers reported being enchanted by the deep connection the indigenous people (the Na'vi) on the planet Pandora had to the Land and to Eywah, its sentient "soul."

After the movie left theatres, a number of news outlets and even academic journals reported on the "Pandora effect" or "Avatar blues." As one viewer said, "When I woke up this morning after watching *Avatar* for the first time yesterday, the world seemed gray. It just seems so meaningless. I still don't really see any reason to keep doing things at all. I live in a dying world." Another fan admitted: "I even contemplate suicide, thinking that if I do it, I will be rebirthed in a world similar to Pandora."[4] Waking up from *Avatar* was a painful experience of disenchantment for some viewers.

Writing in the early 1900s, sociologist Max Weber said that modern life has been a series of such disenchantments. As in the Broadway musical *The Wizard of Oz*, the curtain in the Emerald City has been pulled back. What our ancestors thought was magic and mystery has turned out to be corruption, sleight of hand, or ordinary cause and effect.

While Dorothy's dog Toto did the curtain-pulling in the play, scientists and historians have been our chief disenchanters. Science shows us that we are not the center of all things but brief specks in an unimaginably vast and ancient universe. Historians have unclothed the cast of wizards who populated our national sagas—warriors, priests, kings, entertainers, and athletes—exposing them not as gods but as flawed human beings like (often worse than!) the rest of us. The great religious myths that structured the year and undergirded social values have been unmasked as bedtime stories meant to comfort children or keep them in line. And the Christian churches that claimed to be followers of Jesus participated in the extermination of, or refusal to give sanctuary to, six million of Jesus's Jewish brothers and sisters.

During that twentieth century of disenchantment, some philosophers gloomily described the human condition as meaningless. In his 1903 essay "The Free Man's Worship," Bertrand Russell wrote, "Brief and powerless is Man's life; on him and all his race the slow, sure doom falls pitiless and dark."[5] Similarly, Jean-Paul Sartre lamented in his book *Nausea*, "Here we sit, all of us, eating and drinking to preserve our precious existence and really there is nothing, nothing, absolutely no reason for existing."[6]

Do they need to be so glum? Our cat basks in the sunshine completely untroubled by the possibility that life may have no inherent meaning. But humans are different. Psychologist Carl Jung suggests that humans *need* to know that their lives are purposeful, shaped by a meaningful story. We *hunger* for enchantment.

Why It's Worth Engaging the Tough Questions Anyway

Here then is the modern dilemma: If our virtual realities, our carefully constructed illusions, are necessary for our well-being but so easily destroyed in this era of science, revised histories, and tell-all social media, what are our options? Are we consigned to living either in a fairy-tale bubble on the one hand, or a gray, amoral, aimless existence on the other?

No. There is a third way. Re–enchantment is possible. In my experience one can live with a sense of wonder and delight, a deep appreciation for the beauty and complexity around us, while still honestly acknowledging and trying to address the world's deep pain.

Re-enchantment happens regularly in our family. At every gathering we hearse and rehearse our favorite tales: first dates, epic failures, hilarious absentmindedness, joyful births, and narrow escapes. In the process we are often surprised. New info surfaces as families break up, health wanes, death happens. Cherished assumptions about our heritage are challenged. But we tell the stories anyway—we need them to rebuild family bonds. Even as the stories are revised, they tell us who we are and to whom we belong. They help us become *re-enchanted* with each other.

Something similar is possible with faith communities. Religious re-enchantment happens, but the road to it can be rocky.

This book will take us on that road. We will venture into dark corners of religion that may disgust us; it will take courage to not look away. At the same time, we'll need clear eyes and an open heart to see the sacred that saturates our lives and the land around us because it is so well hidden.

As we take on some tough questions about faith and religion in the twenty-first century, then, there are real risks:

- For you who are believers, becoming more aware of religion's dark realities and its "virtual" character can strip away precious elements of myth and story that have sustained you. It will be *disenchanting*. And it can alienate you from your religious community.

- For you who are not religiously engaged, seeing religion's less savory side may blind you to the quiet, life-giving work of faith communities all over the world. It can inoculate you against *genuine enchantment*.

It's my hope however that if you stick with the questions, you'll find yourself moving through the pain that dogs twenty-first-century religion into a new, more mature form of wonder-filled faith.

Good questions can take us places that simple answers can't

In the chapters to come, we are going to explore the wonder and the woes of twenty-first-century religion through the use of good, tough questions. Good questions are more powerful than simple answers. An answer closes off inquiry and conversation. It's an end. But good questions can open up the world, give us a map for exploring, point the way to hidden treasures.

David Cooperrider and Suresh Srivastva developed the "Appreciative Inquiry" process I mentioned above. The process is based on the insight that organizations grow in the direction of their most frequently asked questions. A school that asks, "How can we keep our children from acting out?" will develop techniques for control. One that asks, "How can we stimulate our children's curiosity?" will become creative and chaotic. A church that asks, "What is wrong with the world (or our youth, or ourselves)?" will become experts on what "sin, death, and the devil" are up to. A church that asks, "What is God doing in the world (or among us)?" will become tuned to that which is life-giving.

Admittedly this book will not be primarily an *appreciative* inquiry. It will ask questions about the misuse of power and beliefs in religious settings. But I will also make an effort to ferret out some of the places where honest faith, re-enchantment, *might* be possible. As we do that, you might want to assess whether the questions the book raises are:

a. *Fair.* Questions can be poorly disguised comments or generalizations: for example, "Why are liberal Christians such pansies?"; "Why are Muslims (or Sikhs) so aggressive?"; "Why are evangelicals so right-wing in their politics?" There are some large assumptions embedded in these questions that a careful examination of the facts may or may not support.

b. *Open-ended.* I've often been frustrated with phone surveys that ask me to choose two alternatives— "either . . . or . . ."—when my response would be a third or fourth option. Good questions recognize that life doesn't fall neatly into dualisms—conservative or liberal, tree-huggers or foresters, black or white. Deeper understanding comes from questions that can't be answered "yes" or "no" but invite us to dig deeper, asking "how" and "what" and "why."

c. *Stretching.* There are several common ways that people develop questions:

i) With a *fence.* Often belief-based organizations define questions as "in-bounds" or "out-of-bounds." A particular congregation, for example, may be able to discuss whether or not communion wine should be served in communal goblets or individual glasses but not whether God exists, or whether religion is a good thing, or whether Jesus ever existed or whether the Bible is reliable. People can explore ideas inside the fence, but outside "there be demons" (heresy).

ii) In *hot air balloons.* Some folks are freethinkers. They are not tied to any creed but float above the world, following the wind currents, getting a bird's-eye view of things. That can be very useful for gaining perspective, but most people don't have the social or financial freedom to live completely untethered. Circumstances force us to pay attention to the gritty, practical requirements of life on the ground.

iii) With *an anchor and a bungy cord.* To meet daily needs in a reliable way, most of us need some anchors, basic working assumptions such as: "parents should protect their children;" "intimate relationships are worth the risk of being hurt;" "everyone should contribute what they can to family/society;" "if I help my neighbor I'll receive help when I need it;" "bad things are going to happen, but I can weather them—I'll be okay in the long run;" and so on. The assumptions may have a religious overlay: "There's a God who knows and cares for me;" "God is all around and I can ask for help anytime;" "trusting God brings me peace." These folks explore ideas using an *anchored bungy cord.* For them a good question is attached to one of their core beliefs, but it stretches them, allows them to explore quite a long way without detaching from their roots.

d. *Alert to the Absurd.* Growing up watching Saturday morning cartoons, I often wondered: If Wile E. Coyote was rich enough to buy all those ACME roadrunner traps (online, in the pre-internet era apparently), why didn't he just order a chicken dinner? It illustrates one more characteristic of good questions—they are often triggered by the absurd or incongruous. (My cartoon musing, for example, might lead us into 1960s capitalism, obsessive compulsive disorder in Arizona coyotes, or the nutritional value of roadrunners.)

Religion too is full of incongruities that raise tough questions. There might be a disconnect between *church* and *workday* cultures. I recall a Pentecostal farmer who said at a rural church conference: "I work mostly with machines or animals, by myself all week. Then I come to church on Sunday and I'm supposed to enjoy standing in a crowd, raising my arms, publicly expressing my emotions, and telling a man [Jesus] that I love him? It's pretty strange!"

There may be a contradiction between *explicit* and *implicit* messages. For example, many churches in our area have "All Are Welcome" signs up outside. But some have steps up to the entrance that bar those with mobility issues. In most there is a divider—an altar rail—at the front that seems to fence the holier folks from the general public. And many churches would not really welcome certain people in their pews—drug dealers, released sex offenders, outspoken gay rights or firearms advocates, the mentally ill, street people, and so on, depending on the congregation.

There may be striking incongruities within sacred stories and beliefs. Some examples from the Christian Bible: In Genesis chapters 1–4, there are only four people in the world (Adam, Eve, Cain, and Abel) but Cain kills Abel then flees to the land of Nod, where apparently there are lots of folks and he gets married; in Deuteronomy 32:18, God is referred to as "the Rock that bore you"—a jarring mixed metaphor; Jesus tells a parable about the mustard seed (Matthew 13:31–32)—which grows up into the largest of trees, sheltering birds (not something I've ever seen in a mustard field!). What's going on in these bizarre stories?

The most shocking incongruities we call "hypocrisy" —deep, intentional departures from a religion's core claims. North Americans are familiar with the damning scandal of Christian churches and church leaders assaulting children in residential schools and parishes—and then going to great lengths to cover up the abuse. It gives lie to the exceptional honor that Jesus gave to children: "Let the little children come to me . . . for it is to *such as these that the kingdom of heaven belongs*" (Matt 19:14). The Middle East has also been rocked by Islamic groups' abuse of children, recruiting them as child soldiers and suicide bombers in spite of the fact that the prophet Muhammad was an orphan who survived only by the kindness of elders and later insisted that adults "*Fear God by treating children fairly*" (Sahih al-Bukhari). How is it possible for religions to harbor, even foster, child abuse and murder?

Being alert to the absurd, incongruous, and hypocritical often leads us into questions that probe the heart of what faith and religion really are—or aren't—about.

Now let's get to the questions!

Explore!

1. Ask someone you know who has been involved in a religious community for a long time the following question: "What would cause you to really re-examine your faith, or your involvement in your religious

group? Has that happened in the past? If so, what caused it? What kept you in, or brought you back into, the group?

2. Tell someone why you picked up this book. What is it that intrigued you? What are you hoping to get out of it? What questions do *you* bring to it?

3. How did you feel about the suggestion that we interact with the world through "virtual reality" interfaces created by our brains and our cultures? How do you feel about the idea that religions are VR constructs too?

Notes

1. For a description of how I use these tools, see Cameron Harder, *Discovering the Other: Asset-based Approaches for Building Community Together* (Lanham, MD: Rowman & Littlefield, 2013).

2. Claudia Willis, "Why Fake Operations Are a Good Thing," *Scientific American* 318, no. 2 (February 2018), 22.

3. "How Fast Are We Moving Through the Universe?" *Science Insider* (in *Business Insider*), May 12, 2016, https://tinyurl.com/yhs5bbcy.

4. Liz Thomas, "The Avatar Effect," *Daily Mail*, January 12, 2010, https://tinyurl.com/yf7t8knf.

5. Bertrand Russell, "The Free Man's Worship," in *Contemplation and Action, 1902-14: The Collected Papers of Bertrand Russell*, vol. 12 (London: Psychology Press, 1993), 72.

6. Jean-Paul Sartre, *La Nausée,* quoted in and translated by Stephen Evans, *Existentialism, the Philosophy of Despair and the Quest for Hope* (Grand Rapids: Zondervan, 1984), 47.

2

Why Bother with Religion? Mystery, Magic, and Miracles

When I was eighteen, I worked for the summer on a pipeline crew. One afternoon I was standing behind the truck cab on a flatbed semi loaded with 4000 lb, 12″ diameter steel pipes. My job was to attach a grappling hook to the front of the top pipe as a large tractor drew up alongside with a boom to lift it off. Unseen by me, the fellow holding the rear grappling hook slipped and fell just as the tractor came alongside. His hook caught the back end of the top pipe and shot it forward like a sling. Standing directly in front of that pipe, I couldn't see what was happening. But suddenly I felt a pressure like a hand on my chest, and I fell backward just as a two-ton pipe zipped across my chin and through the semitrailer cab. The cab driver got out and swore (without repeating himself) for a good two minutes. I was just relieved: If not for that ghostly push I would have been headless.

Religion Grows out of "Mysterious Moments"

Decades later I still don't know what saved me. Was it divine intervention, an angelic hand, a Spirit shove? That's how I like to interpret it, but of course there is no way to know for sure. What I do know is that stories of "mysterious moments" like that are not uncommon. I've heard dozens over the years. Here are a few:

- One elderly woman I visited in a hospital told me her hip broke while she was standing at the sink washing dishes after supper. She fell and spent the night on the floor unable to reach a phone. But she claims that in the night, while she was struggling with pain and fear, an angel came and covered her with a blanket, and she was able to sleep. The next morning, a neighbor looking to share some excess zucchini knocked on the door, found her, and called 911 (another angel!).

- One of our Lutheran chaplains writes about his near-death experience. He collapsed suddenly while leading a worship service and said he was transported to a grassy hill where a figure of profound love and gentle humor met him and assured him that he wasn't alone and still had work to do.

- A young woman who had no religious background or experience whatsoever told me of contracting a deadly cancer in her late twenties. She said that as she was being trundled down the hall of the hospital on a gurney for surgery (prior to being hooked up with drugs), she was unexpectedly embraced by a vast Love that was warm and strong and utterly reliable. "In that moment," she said, "I knew that no matter what happened in surgery, I would be taken care of."

You may have heard stories like this too or have your own to tell.

Similar accounts of mysterious moments appear throughout the sacred writings of Islam, Judaism, Christianity, and, in fact, in almost all religious traditions. In Islam, the Qur'an tells how Muhammad was praying in a cave when a being of power appeared to him, showed him a book, and gave the prophet, who was illiterate, the ability to read it. Judaism tells of the prophet Elijah, who hears the voice of God as a still, small voice calling him back to a ministry of which he had despaired. Christianity recounts the appearance of an angel to Jesus's unwed mother, assuring her that through her son the poor would be raised up and the mighty humbled.

Whether one believes in God or not, anthropologists can attest that every culture has stories of people who randomly, even routinely, have what we might call "spiritual" experiences. In some cases, these experiences become catalysts for the development of new religious expressions in a community. By "religious" I mean any forms of social interaction that involve understanding and interacting with super-human beings (gods, spirits, ancestors, and the like).

Exactly how and why religious expressions took root in human evolution is vigorously debated by scientists.[1] I find social scientist Jonathan Turner's work on the evolution of the human brain interesting. He suggests that our hominid ancestors developed complex emotions and language as a way of building the strong social bonds necessary for survival on the predator-rich African savanna. To reduce conflict with each other and increase cooperative hunting and group protection, rituals developed as key bonding mechanisms.[2] So it is not surprising that when a community member had an unusual experience that hinted at mysterious matters that could affect community survival, the group would tell and retell the story and in some cases embody it in bonding rituals.

In part, the development of religion also reflects our anxiety about the future in a very uncertain world. Scientists tell us our species diverged from the great apes as the African forests diminished and we had to get out of the trees. Standing upright on the savannas made it easier to spot dessert—and danger—at a distance. But it also made oneself a target. That's pretty risky for a species without sharp teeth or claws. So, we worked on seeing ahead not just physically but *temporally*, learning to *predict* what's going to happen so we could better *control it.*

To help with that, our growing neocortex developed the capacity to *imagine* things that didn't actually exist. We imagined technical solutions to secure life such as weapons, and tools for harvesting. We also imagined social categories based on connections between similar things, people, or experiences and mentally tagged them so that one could make better predictions about potential *risks* (enemies), *rewards* (food), or *responsibilities* (family, tribe).[3]

Eventually the category of "powers beyond human control" (gods) was added to that list. The god-language in particular reflected our growing awareness that the universe is, at bottom, a deeply mysterious place.

That mystery generates feelings that are not easy to manage—especially *fear* and *wonder*. It's not that these feelings were new to our hominid ancestors. Jane Goodall documents fear and awe responses in chimpanzees who encounter powerful new forces (see for example their reaction to waterfalls in Goodall's video[4]). But humanity's growing capacity for emotional expression magnified those feelings and made finding social mechanisms to manage and contain such powerful emotions a priority.

Healthy Religion Is Watered by Wonder

I experienced both fear and wonder in an unusually vivid dream one afternoon. I'd lain down on the bed to soak up sunshine and fell asleep. I dreamt I stood on a narrow ledge perched on the side of an impossibly high cliff and surrounded by dense fog. There was no way off the ledge, up or down, no way out that I could see. Gradually I got a sense that I was being watched. I could see no one, but the feeling intensified. I finally realized I *was* being watched—by a vast Awareness, of immense power, that could squash me like a bug if it chose. I became very frightened and looked for a place to hide, but there was none. Crouching down on the ledge, I wrapped my head in my hands and kept perfectly still, hoping to escape notice.

Minutes passed but nothing happened. As I relaxed a bit, I began to recognize that the Awareness was not cold and judgmental but warm, even appreciative. As my body slowly unfolded, that One conveyed to me a deep sense of love and—I'm not sure how to say it—possessiveness, as though I belonged utterly to it. The fear in me transmuted into wonder. I thought: "If this One is *for* me, then why would I ever be afraid again?" Then I woke up.

That experience, and others over the years, have helped me become more aware that the world is a *wonder-full* place. There are certainly dangers, and caution helps keep us alive. But it is the mysteries, the marvels, that really make life full. What is the point of merely protecting a life not really lived, cut off from the wonders that saturate the world around us?

Having children and grandchildren has helped me see more clearly. Children are freshly amazed, not yet numb to the strangeness around them. When I am with them, their delight lets me see spectacular sunsets, tiny insects, starry nights, and bleeding fingers with renewed wonder.

Healthy religion does something similar for us. It doesn't just warn us away from dangerous powers or prepare us for an unknown future. It's not an effort to tame the mystery and make it work for us or persuade (or compel) it to provide us with gifts or protection—though many forms of religion have tried to do that. At its best, religion is hung up on *wonder*. It searches for the signs that there is more to life, more to us, more to the universe, and more of God's goodness in all of it, than we can imagine. Wonder is at the heart of life-building religion. It is the essence of worship.

And wonder is a great source of energy. I've described how I have used Appreciative Inquiry and Asset-mapping to help depressed communities. These planning processes focus not on what is broken, but on what is working *well* in the community and what resources are *actually* available *now* for development. Inevitably, at the end of these exercises, participants express a sense of wonder: "I had no idea that we had so many resources available and such creative people to use them!" "I came in feeling like we were poor; now I know we're rich!" "I can't believe what a positive difference our church is making in this community!" "I couldn't see the amazing things that God is doing in this place." The renewed sense of optimism and energy for strengthening their community is obvious.[5] Before we leave those gatherings, I make sure that we have in place a group scheduled to meet to harness the energy and innovative ideas that have emerged.

Unhealthy Religion Is Fed by Fear

Wonder isn't a natural response, however, when people are under pressure. Our brains have evolved complex systems for understanding and responding to threats.[6] So we give in to fear very quickly. It's much harder to relax into wonder. As a result, many expressions of religion are fear-based. They offer a plan for staying out of hell or for staying in God's good graces so bad things don't happen. But in the process, they cause people to draw into themselves for protection, as I did in my dream, like a turtle into its shell.

Turning inward, we also turn *away* from others. Fear-based religion quickly becomes judgmental. It creates a culture of suspicion and sets up criteria for judgment: "Who is saved, who isn't? Who are the true believers, who are the backsliders and heretics?" Those who follow fear-based religion know that those same questions apply to themselves. So their judgment of others often hides the anxiety they feel internally: "Am *I worthy* of God's favor? Have I done all that I can to get into heaven or stay out of hell?"

Most disturbing to me, the scent of anxiety is a narcotic to those who love power; others' fear gives them leverage. So some residential schoolteachers used religious fears to keep Canadian indigenous children compliant, telling them they would go to hell if they didn't cast off their "savage" culture. And fear has kept churchgoers in the pews of thousands of churches around the world where "hell and brimstone" preachers threatened parishioners with endless afterlife torture if they stopped coming to church and paying their tithes.

Early in my career as a minister, I attended the funeral service of an older man led by one such preacher. He was a big man with a booming voice, dressed all in black. As the sermon began, he stepped out of the pulpit and walked down off the platform to address the four adult sons of the deceased sitting in the front row. Shaking his finger at them, with fire in his eyes and steel in his voice, he thundered, "Your dad is going to hell, and if you boys don't smarten up, you're going there too!"

Many of those present seemed to lap it up (though not the four sons—they were devastated). To an unsettling degree, *fear sells*, not only to the audience ("Wow, what a spectacle!") but often even to the accused ("What if he's right? I'd rather be safe than sorry!"). That preacher, unfortunately, did develop quite a following.

Is that religion? I suppose, but not the kind that gives life. One woman told me that as a child she had been told she was going to go to hell if she didn't measure up. She said, "I decided then that if believing in God means spending my whole life afraid that I'll be tortured forever, belief isn't worth it. I can't live like that."

Clearly then, religion does not always nurture healthy spirituality. And spiritual experiences do not necessarily lead to healthy forms of religion. We can respond to mysterious moments with superstitious fear and religious oppression. Or we can treat them as a window into a wonder-filled world. Our choice.

Does Modern Religion Have Room for Miracles?

In the 1970s, I toured for nine months with a gospel singing/ drama team. Miracle House in Thief River Falls, Minnesota, was one of our stops. During the community's evening worship, a member asked if I wanted my leg healed (one of my legs is longer than the other, which has contributed to serious back problems). Caught up in their enthusiasm, I agreed. While the community sang praise songs with hands lifted, several worshipers sat me on a chair, took hold of my short leg, and pulled hard, praying fervently. To our delight my two heels gradually came together. It was a miracle! We all celebrated the blessing of my bones.

However, the next day, sitting on the floor of my bedroom with hips against the wall, I thought I'd check out the gift I'd been given. To my dismay, my legs were the same unequal length they'd always been. I'd been duped (or I'd fooled myself!). These days I rely on orthotics.

A second story, this one from a professor of mine who had once been pastor of an Alberta parish (I'll call him "Pastor Jim"):

One day a parishioner ("Mike"), asked if Pastor Jim would accompany him to see a Christian faith-healer who was holding meetings nearby. Pastor Jim agreed. When they arrived, the parking lot was crowded, the tent full of the hopeful. There weren't many seats left, but an usher found them two right at the front. He asked if they would like to receive the ministry newsletter, and Mike gave his address.

Not long into the service, the faith-healer invited those who wanted to be healed to come forward. Mike joined the queue. When his turn came, the faith-healer asked what Mike needed to be cured of. Mike replied "smoking." The healer announced in a loud voice, "This man has a demon of nicotine that must be cast out!" and then, without warning he cried, "In the name of Jesus, come out!!" At the same time, he smacked Mike right in the center of the forehead with the palm of his hand.

Mike lurched backward, dizzy from the blow, stumbled down the stage stairs and walked unsteadily toward the back entrance. Concerned, Pastor Jim got up and followed. He watched Mike stagger out to his car, open the glove compartment, pull out a pack of cigarettes and—instinctually to calm himself, Pastor Jim figured—light up and puff away. Pastor Jim told me, "Obviously the healing didn't take. But a week later Mike got a bill in the mail from that faith healer. It said, 'For demon extraction: $13.41.'"

Pros and con artists

As I noted earlier, the world has no shortage of truly "mysterious moments"—extraordinary coincidences, awe-inspiring wonders, inexplicable spiritual encounters, gifts of healing. But it also has no shortage of charlatans. People hunger for wonders, and others happily exploit it—that's the way it's been for thousands of years. Every religious tradition has had its share of shyster shamans, greedy Hindu god-people, corrupt Kabbalists, snake-oil sales-people, Christian TV con artists and their like, with no end in sight.

Americans watched several high-profile debunkings of miracle-workers in the 1980s—Jim Bakker, Jimmy Swaggart, Peter Popoff, and others. In his article "Peter Popoff, the Born-Again Scoundrel" journalist Mark Oppenheimer reviews Popoff's scandal-ridden history. Incredulously, he notes that even after the investigation that led to Johnny Carson exposing Popoff's tricks on the *Tonight Show* in 1986, Popoff barely missed a beat. He found a new (elderly African American) audience that laps up his prosperity gospel promises, and the now seventy-two-year-old Popoff continues to peddle miracles on seven cable TV networks, twenty-three times a week. To his viewers Popoff sends worthless trinkets from China—"revelation stones," "Baruch wallets," and his signature "Miracle Water"—always with a request for money in caps: "REMEMBER YOU MUST SOW THE LARGEST BILL YOU HAVE OR THE LARGEST CHECK YOU CAN WRITE," implying that a large gift to Popoff will cause God to bless the giver with even more wealth. Oppenheimer concludes:

> Peter Popoff is the all-American faith healer because he inhabits both hemispheres of our national brain, the Puritan and the magician. He believes in divine magic—to enrich you, to heal you, or just to entertain you—but not at the expense of the work ethic. He'll do the work, all right, and your part is just suspending disbelief and sending him a check to show that you mean it. He gets rich, you get hope.[7]

So, even if there are *real* miracles hidden among the frauds, can it be a good thing to give them any credence? Our hunger for help in hopeless situations can make us ready to grasp at straws, ready to be taken in by false hope. Then we are crushed when it doesn't pay out.

I visited a young mother ("Mary") in a hospital who had been diagnosed with an incurable cancer and was declining rapidly. During one visit, Mary told me that she had dreamed of a rainbow and that a devout friend ("Sue") told her that this rainbow was a promise that God would heal her. Sue insisted that Mary must not doubt that she would be healed, because unwavering faith was the key.

Next time I saw Mary, we were just concluding our visit when Sue came into the room. I was asking Mary if she had talked with her family about the likelihood of her death and her wishes for the children. Sue jumped in immediately: "That would be doubting! God has promised to heal Mary, but she has to have faith." Mary immediately pulled away from me and said, "Sue is right. I can't think about dying. I saw another rainbow on a poster this morning. It's God's sign—I'm going to be healed."

A week later Mary died. As far as I know she never wavered in her conviction that God would heal her. But she denied her husband and children help in preparing for her death and funeral, and she never came to grips with death herself.

It seems wise to keep a critical eye open when people claim they can deliver miracles on demand because they have some kind of special relationship with, or insight into the mind of, God. Jesus addresses this in a visit to his hometown of Nazareth (Luke 4:16–28). He said (paraphrasing), "I suppose you're going to ask me to do the same things here that you heard that I did in Capernaum" (v. 23). The townspeople undoubtedly nodded. After all, they were better Jews than those mixed-breed folks in Capernaum. They probably thought, "If Jesus is the real McCoy, he should be able to perform even better miracles for us Nazarenes."

But Jesus reminded them that during the great drought and subsequent famine in the days of the prophet Elijah, Elijah was not sent to provide miraculous food to anyone in Israel—just to a foreign widow in the land of Sidon. And while there were many lepers in Israel during the prophet Elisha's time, none of them were healed of their leprosy by Elisha except a heathen army commander—Naaman, a Syrian.

In response to Jesus's impudence, his old neighbors tried to throw him off a cliff. But Jesus had made his point: no one, *especially those who think they are most entitled*, has God in their back pocket. The miraculous does seem to happen, but often in the unlikeliest of times and places, and if such things are God's doing, they are done solely at God's pleasure, not our demand. *No one* has a lock on the power of God (especially those who are most religious).

Another warning signal to watch for around miraculous claims is that of vested interest. Ask yourself, what is this miracle-worker getting out of it? Popoff's payoff was pretty clear: his faith healing spectacles bought him a mansion in California's Bradley Estates (now worth about $10 million), fancy cars, and fame.

In Acts, Simon, a magician, is greatly impressed by the ministry of Peter, a Christian leader. Simon wants in on what appears to be some very powerful action. So, he asks to be baptized into Peter's group and then has a second request. Holding out a few coins Simon says, "Give me this power also, so that anyone on whom I lay my hands may receive the Holy Spirit." Simon thought, perhaps as Popoff insisted, that a little grease on the palms of God's servants would return a large gift from God. But Peter reams out Simon for even asking: "May your silver perish with you, because you thought you could obtain the gift of God with money!" (Acts 8:20).

Of course, the payoff for miracle-workers may come in non-monetary ways as well: fame, social approval, the power to convene and control a group of followers, and so on. Whatever the payoff, there is unavoidable corruption in ministries where one gets rewarded for demonstrating that he or she has God on a leash.

In my opinion, there is no room in our modern world for miracles offered as a last hope to the desperate by the greedy. And there is no need for miracles to prove to others that God exists, or that God is on our side. Miracles can't *prove* anything. If you don't already believe that God indwells the world around us, then you'll likely regard "miracles" as one of two things: (1) natural phenomena for which we haven't yet got an explanation, or which, like cell phones, *I* personally can't explain but other more educated people can; (2) lies or tricks. Either way, the *inexplicable* is not proof of the *Divine*.

The prophet Muhammad knew this. Muslim scholar Faruq Sherif notes that "Muhammad was often challenged—by his critics—to produce miracles; his reply was that God makes miracles appear when He wills, but that the miracles which were performed by the prophets in the past were powerless to convince the people, who treated them as lies and sorcery."[8]

Jesus also knew that every strange occurrence is open to a variety of interpretations. For example, in John 12, Jesus prays to God publicly in the middle of a crowd, and an audible voice responds from the sky. Now, a voice from heaven—you'd think that would surely be proof of Jesus's connection to God, or at least God's existence, or something! But how do those around respond? Verse 29: "The people nearby that heard it said that it thundered. Others said, 'An angel spoke to him.'" A scientific explanation, a superstitious response—but no one except Jesus seems to have interpreted that sound as an "act of God."

It is not only the ambiguity of unusual events that makes such events vulnerable to a variety of interpretations. We are all aware that our human brain is easily deceived. Ever since Moses tried to convince Pharaoh to let his people go by turning his staff into a snake, and the Egyptian court magicians replicated the trick, we have known that our eyes cannot really be trusted. Here is a simple example. Look at the Café Wall Illusion below created by Victoria Skye.[9]

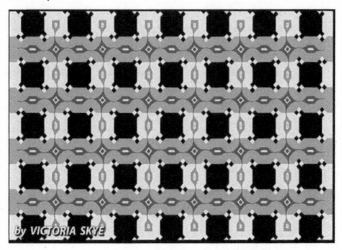

Our mind tells us that the horizontal lines are slanted, but if you measure the distance between the lines at each end (or squint hard) you will see that they are in fact straight and parallel.

Our brains take a lot of shortcuts to help us make sense of the world or avoid danger. They tend to focus on one element in our environment to the exclusion of others, to fill in gaps, to construct familiar images out of unfamiliar arrangements, and so on.

But this means our brains can also be fooled fairly easily. Modern magicians, like David Blaine, Penn and Teller, or Criss Angel, rely on it. Angel often performs on the street without apparent stage props or preparation. In one performance, for example, Angel mixes salt and pepper on a glass restaurant table, then asks a patron to put her hand over the mixture. Angel then slides his own hand under the glass and the pepper seems to seep through the glass into his hand. When the woman removes her hand from over the salt-pepper mixture, only salt remains.[10] It seems miraculous, though of course it's not. But magicians maintain the illusion by carefully guarding the secret of their tricks.[11]

Miracles reveal the sacred in ordinary life

What if one *does* believe in God and is not inclined to attribute all wondrous matters to human ignorance or tricks? Is there a place for miracles in the life of those who have faith? By miracle I mean "God-sightings" or events that more clearly seem to be touched by God in some way. I think there is a place for them, though again, not as proof of the truth of one's religion or its superiority over other religions. (A quick Google search will show that miracles seem to pop up indiscriminately among people of different faiths and people of no particular faith.)

Perhaps the proper role of miracles in the life of believers is a bit like that of volcanoes in modern geology. Until the 1800s when the first seismic readings of the earth were taken, volcanos tended to be regarded as local events, the gods' judgment on the bad behavior of communities (e.g., Moses at Mt. Sinai) or as earthly expressions of conflict between the gods (the Greeks).

Today, thanks to the work of seismologists who can discern the internal structure of the earth through the reflection of seismic waves, we know that the earth has a molten mantle beneath its cool crust. When the plates that compose that crust shift, they allow the earth's fiery magma to spill out in a volcanic eruption. Volcanoes are a cleft in the armor that hides us from the earth's heart. They give us a glimpse of the magmic arteries of 2200F heat flowing under our feet to protect us from the −148F chill of near-earth space. And they remind us that the human life sandwiched between those extremes is very fragile.

Like volcanoes, miracles can be seen by people of faith as a small instance of a much grander marvel. They point to the presence of God—not just in one special moment, but in *every* moment and *every* place, around us, in us, under us, ahead of us. Miracles are cracks in the mask that hides God from our awareness. They point to a God who is *everywhere*, sustaining and recycling life.

It is easy for us to take ordinary life for granted. We don't bat an eye at being able to cram into a tin cigar with 250 other people and fly thirty thousand feet in the air across our planet in a day. We give no thought to the fact that we can stuff all kinds of organic matter into the orifice in our face and by some strange alchemy have it transmuted into muscle and blood. Ordinary life, though it is a complex marvel of communication and interconnection, can easily bore us. Unexpected miracles, mysterious moments, shock us. They open our sleepy eyes to the wonders in which our lives are constantly (though unwittingly) saturated.

Miracles as antidote to fear and despair

Miracles break open the world when it feels like it has closed in—on a grieving widow, on a rural community that has shut down its school, on an indigenous American tribe whose future looks grim. Miracles are moments of hope. They release those whose lives are folded in on themselves, locked into crippling despair, insatiable greed, crushing oppression. They suggest that the future is not predetermined by the "fates" or the markets, by race or gender or genes, but is open to surprise.

In our modern media-saturated world, miracles also serve as a counterbalance to global terror. Once upon a time, the only horrors humans knew about were those that directly touched their personal lives. But thanks to the printing press, and eventually the digital revolution, all the world's horrors are beamed into our living rooms. A steady diet of the news nurtures chronic anxiety. Watching the news, it's hard to imagine that our grandchildren will have a future. But the anxiety simply arises from a sampling error: the media heavily oversample the world's troubles.

Swedish statistician Hans Rosling has a wonderful TED Talk in which he demonstrates how grossly distorted our view of the world is with a simple multiple-choice quiz. He asks questions such as, "On average how many years of education do girls receive globally for every eight years that boys receive?" Or, "In the last 100 years have more, the same, or less people died in natural disasters?"[12] Rosling gives the quiz to Swedish professors, journalists, the American public, his TED Talk audience, and a group of chimpanzees. Guess which group consistently scores the highest? It's the chimps—apparently because they don't watch the evening news and are just guessing randomly. Everyone else dramatically underestimates the well-being that humans are experiencing globally, from the rapid growth in girls' education, to the increase in living standards, and declines in poverty, death by violence and disease, and so on.

Perhaps paying more attention to life's mysterious moments and treating them as a symptom of a divine life undergirding and supporting us, will help to balance our mental scales. Perhaps miracles can help to turn off the "lizard brain" and open us to the wonders around.

Explore!

1. Tell someone close to you about a moment in your life that felt miraculous or mysterious. Ask if they have had a similar experience. Discuss how you interpreted those experiences when they first happened and how you see them now.

2. Try an exercise that shows how your brain attends to things. Go online to "The Monkey Business Illusion" at https://www.youtube.com/watch?v=IGQmdoK_ZfY

and carefully, in sequence without jumping ahead, follow the onscreen instructions. What did you discover about the way your brain processes information and interprets the world?

3. Self-reflection: What makes you feel wonder-*full* (full of wonder)? How does that experience of wonder affect the way you interact with the world? Have you had such experiences in a formal religious setting? What about in the midst of ordinary life?

4. Sit outdoors in a setting where there is more than human habitat. Look closely at the plants, insects, animals, clouds. Focus on one or two of these. Imagine what it is like to *be* that thing. Imagine what the Divine life is *doing* in and through it.

Notes

1. Philip Gorski gives a helpful survey of the theories in his review of Christian Smith's book *Religion: What It Is, How It Works, and Why It Matters*, in "The Origin and Nature of Religion: A Critical Realist View," *Harvard Theological Review* 111, no. 2 (April 2018), 289–304.

2. Jonathan Turner, "Using Neurosociology and Evolutionary Sociology to Explain the Origin and Evolution of Religions," *Journal for the Cognitive Science of Religion* 4, no. 1 (2016), 7–29, https://journals.equinoxpub.com/index.php/JCSR/article/view/35721.

3. This capacity for creating abstract categories has a dark side. When we group people into categories, especially to reduce our risks in interacting with them, we are engaging in race, class, or gender bias. Drawing on social identity theory, biblical theologian and documentary filmmaker Simon Joseph notes, "The mere act of individuals categorizing themselves as group members is sufficient to lead them to display in-group favoritism." "A Social Identity

Approach to the Rhetoric of Apocalyptic Violence in the Sayings Gospel Q," *History of Religions* 57, no. 1 (August 2017), 28–49, p. 42.

4. Jane Goodall Institute, *Waterfall Displays*, Youtube video, accessed Nov 12, 2019 at https://tinyurl.com/wame6jf.

5. Cameron Harder, *Discovering the Other: Asset-based Approaches for Building Community Together* (Lanham, MD: Rowman & Littlefield, 2013).

6. See for example Dean Mobbs et al., "The Ecology of Human Fear: Survival Optimization and the Nervous System," *Frontiers in Neuroscience*, March 18, 2015, https://tinyurl.com/ygn2elpg.

7. Mark Oppenheimer, "Peter Popoff, the Born-Again Scoundrel," *GQ*, February 27, 2017, https://tinyurl.com/yevvbq7t.

8. Faruq Sherif, *A Guide to the Contents of the Qur'an* (Berkshire, UK: Garnet Publishing, 1995), 62–63.

9. Victoria Skye, "Café Wall Illusion," displayed in Cecile Borkhataria, "The Mind-boggling Optical Illusion That Makes Parallel Lines Appear Slanted," Daily Mail.com, August 9, 2017, accessed online November 12, 2019 at https://tinyurl.com/tjymxwf.

10. See Criss Angel, "Criss Angel BeLIEve: Salt n' Pepper (On Spike)," Youtube video, accessed online November 12, 2019 at https://tinyurl.com/yfvafxug.

11. You can see explanations for some of the simpler magic tricks at Mind Warehouse, "World's 7 Greatest Magic Tricks Revealed," Youtube video, accessed online November 12, 2019 at https://tinyurl.com/y8y3ecpx.

12. Hans and Ola Rosling, "How Not to Be Ignorant About the World," Ted Talk, Youtube video, accessed online November 12, 2019 at https://tinyurl.com/mzap7ss.

3

Is It *Good* to Believe in God?
Religion and Violence

One of my workout songs is that oldie by Abba, "I Have a Dream." Remember the line "I have a dream, a fantasy, to help me through reality"? Perhaps that's what belief in God is for many folks—a fantasy, a psychological support that gives them enough hope to make it through dark times.

If so, it's worth noting that not all fairy tales are full of wonder. Some are much more "Grimm." As I'm writing, the world has been shocked by the massacre of twenty-five worshipers in two New Zealand mosques. According to news reports, the shooter had scrawled on his weapons the dates of historic Christian battles. Apparently, he was living out *his* fantasy—a soldier of the Lord waging war like those crusaders of old, slaughtering God's enemies.

Is it religion that makes people do such awful things? In the next few chapters, we will attempt a modest risk assessment of religion. We'll weigh some of the *costs* societies have borne for tolerating religion against the social *benefits* of religion.

That may sound crass, but we make similar cost-benefit calculations about important matters all the time. For example, North Americans in large numbers still choose to form families, despite the fact that between 2000 and 2009 there were about 1500 family-related homicides in Canada[1] and about 25,000 in the United States[2] (and that's not even to mention the much higher prevalence of domestic assaults). On top of that, the majority of marriages end in divorce. It seems that in spite of significant risks to life, limb, and love, we are convinced that the benefits of having domestic partners and stable homes to raise children outweigh those risks.

That sort of risk assessment also applies to government, schools, transportation systems, police forces, and so on. Each of these powerful social institutions has a checkered history. We know (to badly twist an old children's rhyme) that "when they are good, they are very, very good; when they are bad, they are horrid." But we've kept them because, so far, the very, very good seems to outweigh the horrid.

Religion too can be horrid, as we will see examining religion and violence in this chapter and religion and child sexual abuse in the next. In the end we'll have to ask, "Can religion be good enough to keep?"

This type of assessment isn't easy to do in an objective way. First, because it is tough to separate the influence of religion from other social and political influences. And second, because religion and its sometimes-horrid companions trigger strong feelings. Fears can obscure the facts. But we'll take a stab at it, starting with religious violence.

Since suicide bombings have become the iconic form of religious violence in recent decades, let's begin with them. Two questions: How are the bombings related to religion? And what real danger do they pose to our society?

Political scientist Robert Pape studied 315 suicide attacks that took place between 1980 and 2003. In his book *Dying to Win*, he says that media reports about suicide bombings make it seem that the bombers' primary motive was to force their religion on others and exterminate any who resist. What Pape actually found, however, is that the bombing was simply a desperate attempt to repel invaders. Pape writes, "The taproot of suicide terrorism is nationalism—the belief among members of a community that they share a distinct set of ethnic, linguistic, and historical characteristics and are entitled to govern their national homeland without interference from foreigners." Pape concludes, "The data show that *there is little connection between suicide terrorism and Islamic fundamentalism, or any one of the world's religions*"[3] [emphasis mine].

Well, what about the danger? What kind of risk does terrorism pose to Canadians and Americans? Here are a few facts: In Canada, since the Air India Flight 182 bombing in 1985 by Sikh extremists (Canada's largest terrorist attack), there have been only thirty-one people in Canada killed by terrorists. In these cases, as Pape notes, resistance to political and economic oppression is the key motivator. I would add that in some cases mental illness also plays a role.

In the United States, the numbers rise dramatically because of 9/11. But in the eighteen years since 9/11 only 272 Americans have been killed by terrorists, and again the religious component, though difficult to tease out, is not primary.[4] To put the risks in perspective, CATO, a conservative American research institute, calculates that the odds that any particular American will be killed by a terrorist of any stripe are about 1 in 30 million. CATO notes they are *twenty times* more likely to be killed by an animal attack.[5] Or compare the terrorist risk to influenza. In just the one winter of 2017–2018, about forty-nine million Americans contracted the disease, almost one million were hospitalized, and seventy-nine thousand died.[6] Attacks by microbes, not human terrorists, are the real risk for North Americans.

Yet a survey by the Public Religion Research Institute in 2015 revealed that "nearly half (47%) of Americans still say they are *very or somewhat worried* that *they or someone in their family* will be a victim of terrorism" (emphasis mine).[7] So our perceptions of the risks of religious zealotry may be grossly distorted. Perhaps it's because we label as "evil" those threats that come from human sources and are completely outside our control or influence.

Here's the bottom line about religion and violence: like all other powers in our culture (government, schools, family, the economy), religion is a *tool*. It is the skill and intent of the one wielding the tool that determines its effect. For example, a hammer can be used to build homes or take them apart, fix a neighbor's deck, or smash in his head. Similarly, religion can be used to nurture families and communities. It can also be used to incite or justify their destruction.

This is not to say that spiritual traditions are neutral. Just as tools are shaped with a purpose in mind, each tradition has been shaped to suit the needs of the cultures in which it was developed. For the most part, the world's cultures have been patriarchal. So, it's not surprising that strong elements of male dominance (as well as many other forms of dominance) have emerged in almost every spiritual tradition.

What *is* surprising, however, is that these same traditions have also been used to challenge abuses of power in the cultures that birthed them, as we shall see. Women, immigrants, the poor, and many other groups traditionally disadvantaged by their faith community have mined their spiritual traditions to find elements that challenge domineering attitudes and practices. Around the world, those who have suffered from abuse of religious power are introducing new memes and rituals that foster equality.

What Causes the Misuse of Religious Power?

In the years following 911, a number of authors argued that religion was so dangerous that it ought to be eliminated from human society altogether.[8] Hector Avalos, religious studies professor at Iowa State University, in his book *Fighting Words: The Origins of Religious Violence*, even goes so far as to suggest that the US should threaten to destroy sacred centers (he mentions Mecca) as a kind of nuclear deterrent to any religiously connected groups set on harming Americans.[9]

Obviously any such act is much more likely to escalate religious violence than suppress it. But more than that, Jeffrey Seul (Harvard social scientist and specialist in conflict resolution) argues that efforts to erase religion altogether are doomed because religion is so culturally convenient. He says religion serves as a one-stop-shopping-center for the things human individuals and groups need to thrive: big stories that give meaning to life; institutional structures that can organize work toward important goals; moral standards that limit destructive behavior; rituals that create a sense of group identity; and beliefs that give people emotional stability in an unstable, unpredictable world. Other cultural groups can supply some of these—families for example. But religion makes it easy to get them all under one roof.[10]

If Seul is right, then religion is likely here for the long haul; it seems to be one of our favorite "power tools" for building human society. In that case, however, we have a responsibility to know where religious power comes from, how to use it properly, and the ways in which it can be *misused.*

Spiritual traditions are potent for many reasons, but three reasons in particular have historically led to both good and evil.

Religion claims, "We're vulnerable, but God is on our side"

Early in our marriage my wife made a wall hanging that said, "Life is fragile; handle with prayer." The first part is true—all life is contingent, dependent. But perhaps because we are large-lobed, self-conscious storytellers, we humans *think* a lot about our frailty. More than other species perhaps, we pass on our memories of vulnerability in the face of overwhelming forces.

Anthropologists tell us that several of our hominid ancestors (for example the Neanderthals and Denisovans) were driven to extinction, leaving only traces of their existence in our genes. Those extinctions may have been triggered by massive geological changes (for example a super-volcanic eruption in Europe). Even *Homo sapiens* barely survived. At one point we appear to have been reduced to only about 40,000 individuals.

That seems to have left an impression in our genetic memory. Throughout recorded history and still today, fears of "Apocalypse Now"—whether nuclear winter, asteroid impact, plague, earthquake, super-volcano, or the hurricane from hell—inspire our art and literature.

German philosophers from Kant to Schleiermacher, Hegel, and Nietzsche have suggested that this awareness of "ultimate dependence" may also give rise to our sense that there is One *on whom* we are ultimately dependent. Most spiritual traditions acknowledge a Creator from whom we seek and receive all that we need for life. We conclude that because life is fragile it should be handled with *prayer.*

The positive side of knowing that we are dependent has led in most traditions to genuine reverence for the land we share with other species and expressions of profound gratitude to God for the gift of food and shelter that it provides.

On the negative side, being fragile is pretty uncomfortable. We've found it hard to handle for long periods. Religiously, that discomfort shows up in the many apocalyptic stories that pepper most sacred writings. Ecologically, it is reflected in humanity's constant effort to increase our population, our food supply, and technological control of our environment.

The accumulative impact on our planet has been profound. Environmental scientist Jonathan Foley and his team at the University of Minnesota examined a large number of studies that examined the sources of greenhouse gases. They concluded that "agriculture is the largest single source of greenhouse gas emissions. . . . The energy used to grow, process and transport food is a concern, but the vast majority of emissions comes from tropical deforestation, methane released from animals and rice paddies, and nitrous oxide from overfertilized soils."[11]

This ecological violence has been accompanied in Christian theology by a change in the interpretation of Genesis 2:15, where Adam is given responsibility to "till and keep" the garden. Geographical references in the text indicate that the garden is only a small (probably walled) garden on the edge of an "eden"—a mountainous mesa. God's encouragement to humanity to be "fruitful and multiply" is in reference to that small parcel of land. Yet, much Christian theology now speaks of the "stewardship of creation," as if humanity has been given license to expand until we occupy not only the earth but the stars and to turn this entire planet into a food factory for humans.

Again, on the positive side, the "we are fragile, but God is on our side" perspective has been politically hope-infusing for communities beaten down by forces larger than themselves. In the Jewish tradition, it gave energy to their ancestors to seek freedom from slavery. And it had a similar effect on the emancipation of slaves in nineteenth- and twentieth-century North America. In the 1980s it led churches to begin conversations of resistance to totalitarian communism, helping to bring down the Iron Curtain across Europe.

Socially and economically, the "fragile but divinely supported" message has taken practical form as places of worship have become key centers for recovery after the earthquake in Haiti, the Japanese tsunami, and the annual Atlantic hurricanes. And that message is the base for religious nonprofits that provide support for the most fragile—for prisoners transitioning back to society, for victims of rape, drug addiction, and various diseases.

However, religion's claim that God is on our side has unfortunately also been a godsend for political leaders who have borrowed it to bolster their own power and status. They have insisted that God is on *their side in a unique way,* so whatever they decree or do (no matter how violent) has divine sanction. More than a few leaders have portrayed themselves as gods incarnate, for example:

- The Egyptian pharaohs presented themselves as gods to their people.

- Ancient Israelite kings were anointed by religious prophets as God's "chosen."

- Between 42 BCE and 363 CE nine Roman emperors claimed to be gods.

- In seventeenth-century England, King James 1 (of the King James Bible) championed the "Divine Right of Kings," and it became popular in France into the late 1800s.

- Until 1945, Japanese emperors were understood to be the "Sons of Heaven," descended directly from the sun goddess Amaterasu.

- From the time of Charlemagne (c. 800 CE), the Holy Roman Empire, a consolidation of religious and political power centered around the semi-divine status of the emperors, profoundly shaped Western culture.

The tragedy for Western Christianity is that, beginning particularly with Constantine in the fourth century, kings and emperors twisted the faith of the crucified Jesus, the faith of the few and the weak, into a banner for imperial power, a religious cloak for the empire's ambitions to rule the world. So, Christians slaughtered Muslims in the name of Jesus to retake Jerusalem during the Crusades. In the guise of protecting and increasing Jesus's kingdom, thousands of dissidents, Jews, and wealthy landowners were tortured and slaughtered in the Spanish, Portuguese, and Roman inquisitions. And in this past century, Nazi "brownshirts" claimed Jesus's sanction for the holocaust (ironically, since Jesus was a Jew!).

The Christian church worldwide still shows signs of this imperial makeover in the way it elevates a clerical elite and gives them the (often exclusive) right to speak for God.

Religion says "You are God's special people"

As Simon Joseph notes in the article I referred to in chapter 2 on social identity,[12] religious rites and belief systems can be critical bonding agents for maintaining ethnic group identity. Unfortunately, in the process religion can also strengthen tribalism. As a community's internal bonds get stronger, bridges to other communities can be weakened. Other tribes may be branded with negative qualities as a community tries to strengthen its own distinct identity. (An illustration: fans of the Canadian TV series *Corner Gas* will remember how the residents of Dog River spat on the ground when nearby Wullerton was mentioned.)

The greatest damage is done when violence erupts between communities, and the religion that binds each one is held up as a flag of war: "God is on *our* side and *only* ours." Generally, groups go to war to gain land and resources, or to protect those resources from others. But war is costly, mostly to the lowest classes. So, leaders often cast conflict as a divine mandate, making the terrible costs more palatable to the masses. Ironically however, as Mike Martin, researcher in the Department of War Studies at King's College London notes in his book *Why We Fight*, it is very rarely *ideology* (religious or political) that keeps soldiers in the fight. Rather it is their basic human need to *belong* (so they fight for their squad members) and to gain *status* (so they will be respected by their squad and the family at home).[13]

This is not to say, however, that religion itself can't incite violence. For centuries societies believed that because religion was a key source of social glue, only *one* religion could be allowed in each region. Allowing more than one religion, they feared, would result in disunity and social breakdown.

That fear has led to violent persecution of religious minorities. After the sixteenth-century Christian Reformation, German Lutherans slaughtered Mennonites, and French Catholics killed Huguenots. The Pilgrims, whose landing in the New World is celebrated at American Thanksgiving, were fleeing persecution by King James I of England. In this last century, we have witnessed the persecution of Bahá'ís in Iran, Muslims in India, and Hindus in Pakistan; China's repression of the Falun Gong; the massacre of Sikhs in India; Myanmar's attempt to wipe out the Muslim Rohingya; Russia's fierce suppression of Jehovah's Witnesses; and again the Nazis' attempt to exterminate the Jews in the Holocaust. There have been many more such persecutions.

It has not been easy for most societies to embrace the idea that religious diversity can be a strength. And to be honest, that diversity *is* a strength only when the religions involved are somewhat open to one another.

Religion claims "We'll put you in touch with God"

I visited a woman in the hospital (I'll call her "Bev") who said her parents were Lutheran but that she wasn't really a believer. So, I stuck to the practical stuff and asked Bev about her upcoming surgery. It turned out that she was a nurse. Bev spoke about the surgery in a very professional, detached way, giving the impression that it was pretty mundane for her. I concluded the visit by offering, as I always do, to close in prayer. She looked at me and said dryly, "I suppose . . . if it makes you feel better." Not sure how to respond, I just shut my eyes and began to pray.

After a few moments, I felt the bed start to shake. Looking up, I saw that Bev was weeping, quite hard. When she was calmer, I asked what she was feeling. Bev said, "I'm really *afraid*. Being a nurse, I know everything that can go *wrong*. I should be able to handle this. But I can't." The prayer helped Bev open up to what was really going on inside. After that, we were able to have a *real* visit, exploring her anxieties, helping her trust in her medical team—and in God.

That visit illustrates for me what religion's claim to put us in contact with God through prayer is really about. The primary benefit of prayer is not what it does to God, but what it does to the *one who prays*. Prayer *opens* us: to the gracious life of the Creator around us; to what is really going on in our own hearts; to our neighbor who may be in need (or could help us in *our* need or who is giving us trouble); and to the possibility of a better future. Meditation is a form of centering prayer that has a particular focus on openness.

In an article titled "Why People Who Pray Are Healthier Than Those Who Don't," journalist Richard Schiffman reports on several studies that document the role that prayer can have in healing. The studies he reviews found that over 85 percent of those facing a major illness prayed about it, that those who prayed were 40 percent less likely to have high blood pressure than those who didn't, that asthmatic youth who prayed suffered less severe symptoms, that prayer boosts the immune system, and that senior citizens who prayed/meditated lived longer than those who did not.[14]

Somewhat related to healing, prayer also offers individuals and communities a way to express strong emotion cathartically. This can be especially helpful if those feelings might be harmful if repressed, or if expressed in less appropriate venues.

The Psalms are wonderful examples of such prayer. No honest emotion is held back. They range from *depression and lament* ("My heart is like wax. . . . My mouth is dried up like a potsherd. . . . You lay me in the dust of death" Ps 22:14–15), to *shame* ("I am a worm and not human, scorned by others and despised by the people" Ps 22:6), *celebration* ("You turned my mourning into dancing . . . and clothed me with joy" Ps 30:11), *earnest desire* ("Heal me O Lord, for my bones are shaking" Ps 6:2), *gratitude* ("I give thanks to you, O Lord my God, with my whole heart" Ps 86:12), *anger* ("Rouse yourself! Why do you sleep O Lord? . . . Why do you forget our affliction and oppression?" Ps 44:23–24), and even cruel fantasies of *revenge* ("Happy shall they be who take your [Babylon's] little ones and dash them against the rock!" Ps 137:9).

This last psalm is not the only one that expresses an impassioned desire for violence. See, for example, Ps 149:6–7, "Let the high praises of God be in their throats and *two-edged swords in their hands, to execute vengeance* on the nations and punishments on the peoples."

As above, however, the impact of such passages depends on the user. Lest one assume that moderns should expunge every one of them from their sacred scriptures, note the work of Christopher Frechette, who reports on the therapeutic use of such passages with victims of violence. In essence, Frechette says that the scriptures can be used by well-trained therapists to help victims who are believers move away from shame and self-blame, away from a sense of being abandoned by God, to a confidence that God is on their side and God deplores the harm that was done to them. Carefully used, the passages allow the victims to then express their rage in "revenge fantasy"—not by actually *acting* on their revenge, but rather by cathartically giving it to *God* to act on (in the spirit of Romans 12:19, "Beloved, never avenge yourselves, but leave room for the wrath of God, for it is written 'vengeance is *mine*, I will repay, says the Lord'").[15]

These are some of the ways in which religions can put people in touch with the Mysteries—with God and the gods—in positive ways. However, accompanying the traditions around prayer are two elements that have led to forms of violence.

The first is the idea that trusting God with our strong emotions is not enough. In order to really get rid of those feelings, someone has to suffer—often a scapegoat, or sacrifice.

The second is the feeling that God is unaware of our concerns, or doesn't care, and needs to be convinced that our complaints are serious. That has generally been done by our offering (actually, *killing* or *giving away*) something that is valuable to us—again, a *sacrifice*.

René Girard, a French anthropologist, has helped us understand sacrificial patterns and their prevalence around the world.[16] Girard says that when a community is under stress (because of food shortages or war, for example), fear and anger simmer beneath the surface. Instinctively, members realize that if they turn that anger on each other indiscriminately, the community could be destroyed. So, not infrequently throughout history, community leaders have tried to control that destructive energy by focusing it on a common object—often a single member or special group in the community. That person/group then becomes a lightning rod, absorbing the community's anger, releasing the pressure. According to Girard, this is the origin of sacrifice.

Additionally, to distance themselves from responsibility for the violence done to one of their members, community leaders will tell their people that the anger they are feeling is a reflection of *God's anger toward the community*. God must then be *appeased* with a sacrifice. So, a victim is sacrificed in the name of God, relieving the wider community of blame for its misbehavior and of any anxiety about divine punishment.[17]

You might think that sacrificial violence is a relic of the ancient past, but modern religions still show remnants of it. They can scapegoat a particular group of people, laying a community's problems on their shoulders. So, the political rulers in Myanmar identify non-Buddhists as the source of their internal tensions and mercilessly persecute them. In Canada, we have treated our indigenous people that way; in France, the refugees; in America, perhaps black and Latino people. Homosexuals were routinely pointed out as a lightning rod for God's wrath during the AIDS crisis.

Redemptive sacrifice persists probably because it works for a community in the short term (though not of course for the victims!). It unites a community against a common—though artificially constructed—enemy. But it is the easy way out of the community's stress. And it has toxic side effects: redemptive sacrifice teaches a community to address its problems with violence, and it prevents a community from learning the skills it really needs to deal with stress properly or to resolve conflict. In the long run, so-called redemptive sacrifice prevents communities from maturing. And the resentment it generates in the pool of potential victims can lead to violent revolution (the Hunger Games movie series explores this theme).

Explore!

1. Watch with a family member (of an appropriate age) a couple of dramatic TV shows in which the heroes/heroines fix a problem with violence. Jot down a note or two about *how* and *why* the violence seems to be justified in the show's narrative. Discuss: What assumptions are the writers making about the world that justifies the violence? What values do they seem to hold that make violence credible?

2. What did you react to in this chapter? What questions of your own does it raise?

3. If you know someone who works for the police or the military and is an active member of a faith community, ask them how their faith affects their work and vice versa.

Notes

1. Statistics Canada, *Family-related homicides by province and territory, 2000 to 2009*, doc no. 85–224–X, accessed March 18, 2019, https://tinyurl.com/ye89rp5t.

2. US Department of Justice, Bureau of Justice Statistics, *Homicide Trends in the United States, 1980-2008*, by Alexia Cooper and Erica L. Smith, NCJ 236018, November 2011, https://tinyurl.com/y7xylth4.

3. Robert Pape, *Dying to Win: The Strategic Logic of Suicide Terrorism* (New York: Random House, 2005), 79, 4.

4. Max Roser, Mohamed Nagdy, and Hannah Ritchie, "Terrorism," *Our World in Data*, accessed September 11, 2019, https://tinyurl.com/yjknukjz.

5. Alex Nowrasteh, "More Americans Die in Animal Attacks Than in Terrorist Attacks," *Cato Institute*, March 8, 2018,

https://tinyurl.com/yflpxnje.

6. *Centers for Disease Control and Prevention*, "Disease Burden of Influenza," accessed September 26, 2019, https://tinyurl.com/yzbcu3lm.

7. *Public Religion Research Institute*, "Nearly Half of Americans Worried That They or Their Family Will Be a Victim of Terrorism," 2015 American Values Survey, accessed March 18, 2019, https://tinyurl.com/yj6ycwgv.

8. For example: Sam Harris, *The End of Faith: Religion, Terror and the Future of Reason* (New York: WW Norton & Company, 2005); Richard Dawkins, *The God Delusion* (Boston: Houghton Mifflin Co., 2006); Christopher Hitchens, *God Is Not Great: How Religion Poisons Everything* (Toronto: McClelland & Stewart, 2007).

9. Hector Avalos, *Fighting Words: The Origins of Religious Violence* (New York: Prometheus, 2005), 376.

10. Jeffrey Seul, "'Ours Is the Way of God': Religion, Identity and Intergroup Conflict," *Journal of Peace Research*, 36, no. 5 (September 1999), 553–59.

11. Jonathan Foley, "Can We Feed the World, Sustain the Planet?" *Scientific American* 305, no. 5 (November 2011), 60–65, p. 63.

12. Simon J. Joseph, "A Social Identity Approach to the Rhetoric of Apocalyptic Violence in the Sayings Gospel Q," *History of Religions* 57, no. 1 (August 2017), 28–49.

13. Mike Martin, *Why We Fight* (London: Hurst, 2019).

14. Richard Schiffman, "Why People Who Pray Are Healthier Than Those Who Don't," *Huffington Post*, March 19, 2012, https://tinyurl.com/yetsk6b9.

15. Christopher G. Frechette, "Two Biblical Motifs of Divine Violence as Resources for Meaning-Making in Engaging Self-Blame and Rage after Traumatization," *Pastoral Psychology* 66, no. 2 (April 2017), 239–49.

16. For a good introduction to these ideas see Robert Hammerton-Kelly, *Sacred Violence: Paul's Hermeneutic of the Cross* (Minneapolis: Fortress Press, 1991), or René Girard's own *Violence and the Sacred* (London: Athlone Press, 1988). For a description of religions around the world that have used redemptive sacrifice, see *Encyclo-*

pedia Britannica, s.v. "Sacrifice in the Religions of the World." Accessed August 7, 2019, https://tinyurl.com/yfp8syrd.

17. In northern Europe it was often captured soldiers (killed and mutilated), jewelry, treasured weapons, and military vehicles that were sacrificed, then buried in peat bogs for preservation. The National Museum of Denmark in Copenhagen has a compelling display. See also the article by Jacob Mikanowski, "Were the Mysterious Bog People Human Sacrifices?" in *The Atlantic*, March 11, 2016, accessed August 30, 2019, https://tinyurl.com/ygqgrp34.

4

Is It *Good* to Believe in God? Religion and Child Sexual Abuse

About thirty years ago, I was on a plane to the States and got into conversation with the guy next to me. He asked what I did for a living. "I'm a pastor," I said. "What's that?" he asked. "Well, you know, the leader of a Christian church." "Oh, you mean like those guys that were sexually abusing the boys at the Mt. Cashel Orphanage in Newfoundland?" As we talked, I realized this fellow knew virtually nothing about religion—except one thing: it can lead to the sexual abuse of children.

The stories of survivors that have been emerging from investigations of child sexual abuse by Catholic priests in Boston and other places in the United States, Canada, Ireland, Australia, and other countries are heart-breaking. I was devastated by the stories of Indian Residential School survivors in Canada (most run by various Christian denominations) that I heard at the national Truth and Reconciliation Commission gatherings in 2008 to

2015. Describing his own experience, commissioner Dennis Whitebird, for example, says:

> You have 100 beds in one dormitory all squished together and the priests and the nuns and the other lay missionaries going from bed to bed. You'd lie still and pretend to be sleeping when something like that was happening and you wanted to make sure you weren't the next person. There was physical and sexual abuse that was also happening in showers and there were even some (students) that were taken out of their beds and taken into the supervisor's sleeping quarters. It was rampant. . . . For myself, I carry a lot of emotional baggage and you are almost like a walking time bomb that's going to explode at any time.[1]

While the relationship between religion and violence in general is important, the particular connection between religion and child sexual abuse is crucial for many. Sexual abusers of children may currently be the most viscerally hated group in the Western world, to the extent that they are despised even by murderers and drug dealers in prison. So, if it turns out that religion is a special spawning ground for such people, is it perhaps best to turn our backs and walk away from religion?

To find out, we need some data: How is child sexual abuse ("CSA" for short) defined, and by whom? What is the rate of CSA in the general population, and how does it compare to the rate in religious institutions? Is CSA dealt with differently in religious settings than in other settings? If so, why? And what are the current trends? Is the problem getting better or worse? If we can get some reliable information on what is actually happening, then it may be possible to at least tentatively explore questions about the root causes of CSA, religious or otherwise.

As you might imagine, however, it is not easy to get solid facts in this area. Child sexual abuse generates a lot of shame in every culture, so much goes unreported. Children are often alone with abusers and easily intimidated into silence. They may not be aware, cognitively at least, that what is being done to them is *wrong*. Even if they hate it, children may feel guilty, thinking that they are somehow to blame. And they often don't have the language to describe their experience. So, children may not tell adults, or if they do, adults may dismiss their stories as fantasy. Even when responsible people blow the whistle, officials may be quick to conceal the problem to protect their institution's reputation. High-profile cases such as Mt. Cashel Orphanage in Canada or the Boy Scouts of America show how well and how long cover-ups can be maintained.

As a result, CSA incidence reports (e.g., formal complaints to police or institutional officials) are far lower than prevalence research indicates. Prevalence stats are derived primarily from direct interviews with adults about their personal experience of CSA when they were children. So, they report on many incidents that were never officially recorded. Unfortunately, comprehensive, rigorous prevalence research is still in its early days in most countries.

I have to admit that I'm also personally biased; I have had family, friends, and colleagues I care about suffer lifelong consequences from being sexually abused as children, both inside and outside of religious settings. I have also worked with CSA offenders. And I have grandchildren I want to protect. So, the matter is close to my heart, and it would be easy for me to simply vent. However, I have noticed that most media attention to this matter is saturated with anger and disgust but rarely offers much solid data or useful insight. So, I will simply try to share the best of the research that I have uncovered, recognizing that the data is not always clear or complete.

Defining Child Sexual Abuse

World cultures vary in what forms of intimacy they will accept with children. Generally, sexual interaction between men and boys is prohibited. But otherwise there is fairly wide latitude for sexual contact between adults and children in some Caribbean and Asian countries.[2]

For our purposes, however, I find the American Psychological Association's definition of child sexual abuse helpful. It insists that the core of true CSA is "the *dominant position* of an adult [and I would add "or significantly older child"] that allows him or her to *force* or *coerce* a child into sexual activity." That activity might include contact with the child or adult's genitals; anal, vaginal, or oral-genital penetration; unwanted kissing or fondling; or non-contact abuse through sexual propositions, or exposure to an exhibitionist or to sexual videos and materials or child pornography.[3]

How Prevalent Is Child Sexual Abuse?

The true prevalence of CSA is difficult to assess, as every researcher notes. But there is a growing consensus that CSA is *widespread in every sense*: globally, among institutions and religious groups, among genders and ages.

In 2011, a comprehensive global meta-study of CSA was carried out by Marije Stoltenborgh and her team at Erasmus University in Rotterdam. It analyzed the results of 331 regional studies worldwide, involving almost ten million participants.[4] Participants were interviewed as adults and asked if they had experienced sexual abuse (clearly defined) as children. There was wide variation between countries in the results, especially for boys who, for example in Africa, reported CSA at rates ranging from 5 percent to over 50 percent.

The bottom line for Canada and the United States is that on average about 20 percent of females and 8 percent of males report (as adults) that they were sexually abused as children. This is very close to the overall world average. Imagine the social, emotional, and economic cost when one out of every five to ten citizens in our countries is carrying what Whitebird called "a walking time bomb" in their chest!

The difficulty for our question is that prevalence studies have not yet been able to tease out the role that *religion as such* plays in CSA because it is tangled with other factors such as institutional management styles, socio-economic class, family stability, and so on. What is quite clear however is that in all countries most of the abuse takes place first in homes (especially for girls) and then (especially for boys) in institutions and clubs that work with children. There is also more sexual abuse of children when the adults that supervise them are in the eighteen- to thirty-five-year range, when there are fewer adults and more children, and when direct oversight of the adults is lax or missing. Apart from those generalizations, however, studies of CSA show enormous variance. In this chapter I think that the best I can offer will be to provide some insight into the *impact* that CSA in religious settings has on children, the factors that influence religious abusers, and the response of religious organizations to CSA.

Impact of Child Sexual Abuse in Religious Settings

Observation and interviews show that any two children may respond to the same form of sexual abuse in different ways. Any child's specific reaction depends on several factors: the child's gender and personality; their relationship to the offender; how the offender keeps the child quiet; how often the violation is repeated; the support (or lack of it) from family and friends; and so on.

However, it is safe to say that only in rare cases is there no significant impact. Often the effects are severe. A large American study of 17,337 adult Health Maintenance Organization (HMO) members found that adults who had experienced sexual abuse as children were more than twice as likely to have attempted suicide and had a 40 percent increased risk of marrying an alcoholic and a 50 percent increased risk of having current problems in their marriage.[5] Other studies have noted high incidences of anxiety disorders and substance abuse in survivors.[6] And PTSD reactions are common—57 percent according to the review of studies by Martine Hébert and colleagues.[7]

Those related to the victim suffer too. When CSA is publicly reported, it sends out ripples of anger and shame that fracture relationships between family, friends, work colleagues, and institutional staff and members. "Sides" often form in support of victims and alleged abusers, creating rifts that may not heal for decades after the abuse has been officially dealt with.

The ripples also extend across generations. An Australian Royal Commission (ARC) completed a massive investigation into CSA in Australian institutions. It notes the intergenerational effects: "Children of some survivors have been exposed to the debilitating effects of trauma on their parents and families, including mental health and relationship difficulties, alcohol and drug abuse, and family breakdown. In some cases . . . these effects can span multiple generations, perpetuating cycles of disadvantage and trauma."[8] At the Canadian Truth and Reconciliation gatherings, the children of Indian Residential School survivors told us how the destructive patterns their parents experienced were being replayed in their own lives.

One survivor sums up their experience of CSA in an interview with the Australian Royal Commission: "As a victim, I can tell you the memories, sense of guilt, shame and anger live with you every day. It destroys your faith in people, your will to achieve, to love, and one's ability to cope with normal everyday living."[9]

Saddest of all, most young victims suffer these things in silence. Statistics Canada, referring to child abuse in general (not just sexual, which might be worse), reports, "The vast majority of victims (93%) of childhood physical and/or sexual abuse did not speak to either the police or child protection services about their experiences before they turned 15. About two-thirds of victims (67%) did not speak to anyone, including friends or family."[10] In the Australian studies, the average time between incident and reporting was *twenty-three years!*[11]

There can be gender differences. Most studies found that boys were more reluctant to report than girls. Some studies found they expressed greater fear of the abuser's threats than girls, had less confidence they would be believed, and worried that others would think they were homosexual if the abuser was male. Girls also suffered silently, in part because they were frightened, but often because they felt guilty or did not want to hurt the abuser. Girls also tended to play down the importance of the abuse ("it didn't bother me that much"), perhaps implying that abuse was the sort of thing females could expect.[12] Every failure to report, however, means that children suffer longer and more repeatedly, and more children are abused.

If the abuse takes place in a religious institution, and especially if the abuser is a religious leader, similar dynamics apply. However, two elements are intensified. First, the impact on the child's *faith* is magnified. The child may experience a profound loss of trust in God,[13] even feeling that they have been abused by God and feeling guilty that they have somehow caused a "holy" person to stumble and fall.[14] Children say they think God has forgotten or is punishing them. And sometimes, to protect themselves from such feelings, they simply stop believing that God exists.[15] Child psychologist Donald Walker notes that some survivors "never prayed or attended a religious service again."[16]

Secondly, children in religious communities have historically tended to get less support when reporting CSA than children in other abuse groups (for example victims in schools or foster homes) and therefore feel betrayed by and alienated from their faith groups. Later in the chapter we will look at some of the uniquely religious elements that contribute to the failure of some religious organizations to respond to CSA.

Who Are the Abusers?

On October 27, 2018, the Prime Minister of Australia, Scott Morrison, responded to their Royal Commission's report on the investigation of seventeen thousand CSA survivors. This is part of what he said in his apology:

> As a nation, we failed them, we forsook them, and that will always be our shame. . . . The crimes of ritual sexual abuse happened in schools, churches, youth groups, scout troops, orphanages, foster homes, sporting clubs, group homes, charities, and in family homes.

Morrison makes a crucial point—that the problem of child sexual abuse is not just perpetrated by a few hundred twisted people. It's easy to load all the guilt and shame of CSA onto a few offenders and dump our anger by consigning them to hell or a penitentiary. Scapegoats are always popular; those who sexually abuse children are easy to hate. But scapegoating doesn't protect the *next* child from abuse. Truth is, it's *we*—our families, communities, our entire nation—who fail our children because they are being abused on *our watch*, under our noses. We have failed to protect them.

To keep our kids safer, we need to know something about their abusers. My research into the perpetrators of CSA confirmed some common stereotypes, but it held some surprises too.

- *Abusers are mostly not pedophiles.* First of all, the term "pedophile" properly describes only those whose primary sexual interest is *pre-adolescent* children. Those sexually interested in *adolescents* are technically referred to as "ephebophiles." But secondly, it turns out that the vast majority of those who abuse *do not seem to prefer children sexually.* The large-scale John Jay College of Criminal Justice study of Roman Catholic abusers, led by Karen Terry, found for example that "less than 5 percent of the priests with allegations of abuse exhibited behavior consistent with a diagnosis of pedophilia."[17] It seems that abusers are motivated by needs other than sex.

- *Abusers are mostly not serial predators.* The John Jay report also found that more than half of Catholic clergy abusers had just *one* known victim (there could be more, of course), with the average being three. They found a wide spectrum of abusers, from those who kissed or touched an older teen once in a situation of unplanned intimacy, to a small number of true predators who had many carefully groomed pre-pubescent victims.[18] It suggests that not all offenders should get the same treatment.

- *Those who abuse children of their own gender are not necessarily homosexual.* A major US study of CSA in schools notes for example that "of the 24 percent of males who targeted other males, all of the offenders described themselves as heterosexual, with most living in married or heterosexual relationships."[19]

- *Religious celibacy contributes but is a minor cause.* CSA occurs across the board in religious and nonreligious organizations, most of which do not practice celibacy. And only a small minority of celibates actually abuse children. However, the Australian commission notes that celibacy can become an "impossible ideal" that religious leaders can't, and therefore don't, live up to. In some situations then, violating these vows can come to be seen as unavoidable and excusable, allowing sex not only with adults, but also with children.[20]

- *Abusers are generally well known to victims*—74 percent, according to the US Department of Justice study.[21] This makes sense. Those who cross the line once, or accidentally, are most likely to do it in a close relationship, where loving touch and tender words are not only appropriate but necessary for children's well-being. And it is much easier for a true predator to "groom" a child for an assault if they have *legitimate* access to the child.[22] This is the terrible irony—that the people most dangerous to children are their caregivers. Children are most at risk where they *live* (family, daycare, foster home, or residential school), where they *learn* (school, skill tutors), where they *worship* (churches), where they *play* (sports, youth groups, camps), and where they *heal* (medical clinics, hospitals).

- *Criminal record checks generally don't work.* In the past (not so much today) allegations of sexual abuse were handled "in-house" by institutions, so nothing shows up in police records. Yet record checks are routinely required, while more effective strategies—such as putting in place a two-person leadership policy that ensures that no adult is alone with a child—are ignored. Does that suggest that some organizations may be more concerned with protecting themselves from lawsuits than protecting children from abusers?

- *Abusers are both male and female.* In most studies 80 to 90 percent of CSA incident reports are about male offenders. However, a major prevalence study by the US Department of Education in 2004 found that when adults were asked if they had been sexually abused as children in school, 57 percent of those who said they had been abused reported a male offender and 43 percent mentioned a female offender. Since *96 percent* of those *investigated for CSA* in school settings are male, it suggests that female offenders may be highly underreported.[23]

- *Religious offenders show up in all faith groups.* The United States, for example, is predominantly Protestant and, despite what one sees in the media, the majority of religious CSA offenders in the United States are in fact Protestant. The study by the John Jay College of Criminal Justice found that Catholic priests and Protestant ministers also harbor similar percentages of abusers. About 4 percent of American Catholic priests who served between 1950 and 2002 were accused of CSA.[24] Studies by Thomas Plante and Cynthia Doxey did not find this to be higher on average than other religious groups in the United States.[25] Media may focus on the Catholic Church because it is a global entity with a single face that is easier to identify (and to sue) than the fragmented groups of other traditions.

- *Abusers have often been victims themselves.* CSA offenders are *more* likely than the general population to have been sexually abused (up to 40 percent in one Canadian study). However, the majority of CSA offenders have not been victims. And being a victim does not make it likely that one will become an abuser.

- *Abusers are much more likely to be narcissists than sociopaths.* Abusers tend to view their sexual acts only in terms of how those acts affect themselves. Andrew Denny found that clergy who engaged in sexual misconduct in Protestant churches had higher than normal levels of narcissism (using Raskin and Hall's 1979 Narcissistic Personality Inventory).[26] In my own work with sex offenders, I have found that most tend to lack any real insight into the impact of their actions. They are primarily concerned with how they themselves feel—excited, comforted, powerful, guilty—as a result of their sexual behavior and how any exposure of their actions will affect their public image. They cannot seem to put themselves in the child's place, and if they do, they rationalize that the child enjoys or even needs the attention.

- *Power and proximity are the best predictors of abuse.* Why do abusers do it? Because they *can.* Easy access to children and power over them seem to be the only two truly common factors regarding offenders in the various studies. Some situations concentrate power and proximity—family homes of course but also home substitutes. Private, British-style boarding schools have a particularly bad reputation because they create 24-7 opportunities for private "tutoring" or "discipline" and put children into dormitories where older children and staff have easy access at night.[27] The residential schools for indigenous children in Canada (where they were run by twelve different Christian denominations) and in Australia (where the schools were mostly Catholic or Anglican) provided innumerable opportunities for abuse. Small numbers of staff and large numbers of children created many occasions when staff could abuse children away from prying eyes. And it reduced the number of adults available to monitor children's abuse of each other.

How Does Religion Affect Child Sexual Abuse?

As I indicated, it is not easy to tell whether the *rate* of CSA in religious institutions is higher or lower than others. However, there are several factors particularly at play in religious settings.

Saving face

As I was writing, CBC news broke the story that a boy had been sodomized with a broom handle by a group of older boys at St. Michael's Catholic high school in Toronto (November 10–17, 2018). Several other instances of severe bullying at the school emerged shortly afterward.

When the story first emerged, parents whom I saw interviewed on TV were very angry at the CBC reporter. They didn't seem shocked by the story itself or especially concerned for their children's safety. Rather they were offended that this private school, with its reputation for producing leaders in business, politics, and other fields, had its good name dragged through the mud. The school itself had been quick to report to police. But parents seemed to wish they hadn't. After all, parents paid good money to send their child to a private school so he or she would have a better chance at getting into a high-ranking college. If the school's reputation was damaged, donations would decrease—raising tuition for parents—and prospective colleges might no longer regard the school's graduates (their child!) with the same esteem.

In all institutional settings, but especially those that are religious, there are strong pressures to avoid scandal. Like other nonprofits, religious groups rely on the goodwill of donors for their financial survival. So, scandal threatens their existence. But unlike other nonprofits, religious groups often present themselves as keepers of their society's core values and morals (this is one reason why they get tax exemptions in the United States and

Canada). So public shame is ramped up when an abuse happens in a religious setting. This is especially true in rural towns where the worship center is regarded with a certain amount of pride ("it shows we are a *good, safe* place to live").

But when these spiritual custodians of a community are alleged to be harming its most precious resource—their children—the character of the whole community is called into question. So, religious scandals can generate *communal shame* and pushback in the form of communal denial. Rex Murphy, an acerbic Canadian columnist from Newfoundland, said when the Mt. Cashel Orphanage scandal broke:

> [This scandal] posed questions that were absolutely fundamental to Newfoundland's self-image. . . . We have such shocking politics and economics—I think we clung on to the idea that we had a bit of decent domestic or personal virtue and this thing just blasted that all to hell. . . . So, it was yes, at the core, a story with a religious dimension, but it had an awful lot more wings . . . than just religious.[28]

To avoid the shame, Newfoundland police, bishops, and media colluded to sweep the Mt. Cashel scandal under the rug.

Sadly, in the effort to protect their church, members end up *revictimizing* children as, like the abuser, they try to suppress children's voices. For example, CSA victims among Jehovah's Witnesses and the Jewish Yeshivas in Australia were told by elders that those who tried to discuss the abuse with others, or tried to leave the organization, would be shunned—that is, no one in their religious community (including family) would have any dealings with them. Even when the charges were later proven publicly, elders refused to offer apologies. In another shocking example, "Amanda," a member of an independent Australian Christian church, was *beaten by her mother* when she refused to participate in, and tried to expose, the religious leader's repeated sexual "exorcisms."[29]

Clerical entitlement

Most religious bodies have a group of revered "holy ones"—priests, prophets, gurus, or shamans—who have special training and spiritual experience. Members believe that these holy ones can put people in touch with God—even speak *for* God. When religion is functioning well, these folks serve as catalysts and trainers for the spiritual development of all. When it is functioning badly, a lot of *power* becomes vested in that holy one, not only in their position, but also in their *person*.

Tibetan Buddhism is currently struggling with this. Key leaders of the popular Shambala and Rigpa Buddhist communities (including Sogyal Rinpoche, perhaps the world's best-known Buddhist teacher next to the Dalai Lama) have been facing sexual abuse allegations that include children for decades. According to journalist Joe Shute, Rinpoche "claims to offer the attainment of spiritual enlightenment in a single lifetime." The catch: "The student gives total obedience to the lama—a bond which, if broken, is believed to result in banishment to 'vajra hell,' an infinity of unfortunate rebirths."[30] Obviously reporting sexual assault is difficult for victims with that sort of eternal threat hanging over them.

Clerical power is also a significant CSA factor in Protestant Christian megachurches, where it is a function of congregational size and a lack of oversight by regional authorities. Glenn Starks, in his study of sexual misconduct in mega-churches, notes how the abusive pattern develops:

> When these churches are founded, they have small memberships and the church leader is under scrutiny. As the church grows so do leaders' popularity, power, and propensity to adopt more secular behavior. At the same time, their egos grow, making them feel more invincible in terms of scrutiny and freedom to take liberties.[31]

The power seduces clergy into believing not only that they can *take what they want* without fear of punishment, but also that they are *entitled* to take what they want. That entitlement makes it easier for them to separate their "walk" from their "talk." Starks mentions Pastor Eddie Long, who launched a high-profile religious battle against homosexuals while simultaneously engaging in sex with at least four adolescent boys on repeated occasions.[32]

"Not of this world" beliefs

Many religious groups hold that they are God's chosen people, God's kingdom on earth. Therefore, they believe, they are accountable primarily to God, not to secular authorities. Small or persecuted religious groups may see themselves as a "faithful remnant" in a corrupt world and insist on handling all issues in-house. For example, the small Australian Jewish Yeshivas operate under the concept of "mesirah," which prohibits a Jew from informing on another Jew or handing them over to civil authorities.[33] Buddhist reporter Mary Finnegan notes similar behavior in Buddhist monasteries: "The rule in lama land is that you never air your grievances to the outside world."[34]

Some religious groups that are large and strong see themselves as self-sufficient—God's "kingdom" on earth. This may be true of the global Roman Catholic Church. According to the Australian commission, between 1990 and 2010, the Pope's office restricted bishops from reporting allegations of CSA by clergy to the police and insisted that its own "canon law" be treated as the ultimate authority.[35]

Small or large, religious groups with a "not of this world" mentality are reluctant to report CSA offenses to police. For them, to go outside the group is seen as extreme disloyalty that can result in whistle-blowers being disciplined by their religious community.

A purity ethic

One offender said to me, "I'll never get this stain off my soul. I feel so dirty." Never once, however, did I hear that person express sorrow for, or any real insight into, the harm done to their victims. This is characteristic of the narcissism that many serial offenders display. But it is also a result of the tendency toward moralism in some religious communities. They get caught up in striving for personal purity based on perfect behavior instead of nurturing healthy relationships and healing the broken.

Sexual abusers gravitate to a purity ethic. It keeps them focused on their own needs (for gratification, secrecy, reassurance, forgiveness, exoneration) so they can ignore how their actions are damaging a child. If caught, the abuser will tend to present themselves as the victim of unjust accusations, intensifying the focus on themselves.

That ethic is reinforced by religious communities who may feel that if a religious leader is found to be "impure," it will compromise the integrity of the community's worship and ministry for the entire time the leader has been in office. So, when a charge of CSA comes up, those groups focus on hiding or amending the behavior of the abuser, rather than on the victim's injury.

Of course, malicious accusations of CSA *do* occur (and are devastating to the family and career of those falsely accused). So careful investigation is necessary by police and church officials to get at the truth. But too often, this means that again the accused remains front and center, the victim forgotten.

Cheap mercy

One woman said, referring to her pastor's crime in the context of his whole ministry: "It's just one drop of ink in crystal clear water."[36] Religious communities can develop a deep emotional intimacy with their leaders. So even if parishioners acknowledge that harm was done, some may feel that the harm is offset by their leader's good deeds, and they are quick to offer the abuser forgiveness, a "second chance."

However, such offers are not true mercy if there has been no accountability before courts or victims. When an organization quickly extends forgiveness to an abuser, bypassing the actual victim, it lets the organization off the hook. The scandal is quickly cleared away. And by keeping the focus on the abuser, the organization doesn't have to account for its failure to set clear boundaries and monitor those who interact with their children. No true reconciliation—with victim or community—takes place.

Most tragically, the *victim is* forgotten, abandoned to their pain and shame. No healing of relationships or the child takes place. *In the end, the abuser may be restored to heaven, but the victim is left in hell.*

Secret-keeping

In spite of widespread conversation about sexual matters in the media today, sexual behavior for a long time was hidden behind a privacy screen. This is still true in some religious traditions, especially those where sex, as such, is regarded as something shameful or dirty. A "cone of silence" is lowered over sexual matters. This has a double effect. Children who have not been appropriately instructed about body boundaries and appropriate intimate contact do not always realize that they are being sexually abused. So they say nothing. And while adults may confess a sexual problem to their religious leader, they expect the leader to keep strict confidence about it.

As a result, if a leader's sexual misbehavior is discovered, the leader may feel justified in invoking that same cone of silence, expecting parishioners to keep their secret in return. In some

Catholic jurisdictions, abusers have relied on the sanctity of con-fession to (other) priests as a kind of steam valve—releasing the pressure of guilt so they can abuse again. One abuser said, "In a strange way the sacramental confession let us off the hook rather lightly, and perhaps allowed us to minimize what was really hap-pening."[37]

Of course, clergy are not the only professionals that have to deal with confidentiality—lawyers, accountants, medical profes-sionals, and counselors do as well. But as common sense would dictate, when they see that a crime is being committed—a child injured, a firm laundering money, a terrorist trying to avoid prosecution—most report it and are protected in doing so. Reli-gious jurisdictions are following suit, but more slowly.

What Is the Trend for Child Sexual Abuse in Religious Settings?

There's hope. Data from several countries indicates that child sexual assault incidents are sharply declining. They peaked in the 1960s and '70s. In 1984, the largest Canadian study done to that point revealed that about 40 percent of girls and 28 percent of boys had been victims of unwanted sexual acts.[38] But twenty-seven years later, an analysis of twenty-two thousand respondents to the Canadian community health survey shows that rate had been cut in half in Canada.[39]

Even more interesting is that numerous studies in Canada, the United States, and, in fact around the globe, show that the inci-dence of sexual assaults against children ages seven to thirteen grew rapidly after World War II, peaking in the '70s but declin-ing rapidly after 1992.

It is impossible to know exactly why this period resulted in so many cases of CSA. But there is an interesting correspondence with the postwar baby boom. By the early '50s, our two countries were faced with large numbers of children that needed to be trained in sports, faith, and education. Children's clubs, camps, and ministries sprang up everywhere. A heady spirit of unlimited growth was in the air. Burgeoning new congregations sprouted up in every city suburb.

However, the number of adults available to care for these children (and to supervise the caregivers) had been sharply reduced by war losses. And many of those adults had been hurt psychologically and spiritually by the war.

What this meant for CSA is that after the war, there were fewer adults—many emotionally wounded—looking after a very large number of children, with much less oversight and likelihood of detection, than at any time in modern history. And when that great group of children reached adulthood in the '60s and '70s, a portion of them (perhaps larger than usual because so many of *them* were abused) in turn became abusers, continuing the high CSA incidence into the '80s and '90s.

Churches, and most institutions, for some of the reasons above, were sadly slow to recognize the problem and develop ways to handle it. Thankfully, careful and courageous work by survivors, researchers, compassionate churches, school and medical professionals, and the media brought CSA into the spotlight early in this new century. All accredited training schools for religious professionals now teach students how to respect boundaries and to spot boundary-crossers. Many congregations now have formal policies on how to protect the vulnerable.[40] Parents are much more likely to help their children develop body awareness and clear rules for reporting boundary-crossing. Volunteer organizations have strengthened their screening and supervision of volunteers. And legislation has been beefed up to ensure that abusers are dealt with fairly but firmly.

Explore!

1. What in this chapter surprised you or angered you? Go to the place in the chapter where those feelings were triggered. See if there is an associated endnote with a web address. Check out the website for more information.

2. Talk to the head of an institution you are connected to that works with children (e.g., a school, daycare, sports team, hospital, religious organization, children's club, etc.). Ask them if they have a written policy on the protection of children from sexual and other kinds of abuse. Ask them how that policy is communicated and put into action. Read the policy and ask yourself, "Does this policy fit the cultural and practical realities of the children it is trying to protect? Does it seem like it would be effective?"

3. Talk with extended family about what they do to ensure that their children are protected. What do they say to the children about body boundaries and good touch? What do they look into when signing kids up for ballet lessons or Hebrew school? What might they notice in their child's behavior or demeanor that would lead them to investigate the possibility of abuse?

Notes

1. Dave Chan, "Residential school survivors and their descendants share their stories," *The Globe and Mail*, updated May 15, 2018, https://tinyurl.com/ykxs7orb.

2. To read more, see Helen Noh Ahn and Neil Gilbert, "Cultural Diversity and Sexual Abuse Prevention," *Social Service Review* 66, no. 3 (September 1992), 410–27, pp. 411, 415, 422 or UNICEF

Office for Barbados and the Eastern Caribbean, *Child Sexual Abuse in the Eastern Caribbean*, by Adele D. Jones and Ena Trotman, 2010, accessed online November 13, 2019 at https://tinyurl.com/yx5uj9h5.

3. Theo Gavrielides, "Clergy Child Sexual Abuse and the Restorative Justice Dialogue," *Journal of Church and State* 55, no. 4 (Autumn 2012), 617–39, p. 617.

4. Marije Stoltenborgh et al., "A Global Perspective on Child Sexual Abuse: Meta-Analysis of Prevalence Around the World," *Child Maltreatment* 16, no. 2 (2011): 79–101.

5. Shanta R. Dube et al., "Long-Term Consequences of Childhood Sexual Abuse by Gender of Victim," *American Journal of Preventative Medicine* 28, no. 5 (June 2005), 430–38, https://tinyurl.com/w735ke5.

6. Alan Carr et al., "Adult adjustment of survivors of institutional child abuse in Ireland," *Child Abuse and Neglect* 34, no. 7 (2010), 477–89, https://tinyurl.com/spau36g.

7. Martine Hébert, Francine Lavoie and Martin Blais, "Post Traumatic Stress Disorder/PTSD in adolescent victims of sexual abuse: Resilience and social support as protection factors," *Ciência & Saúde Coletiva* 19, no. 3 (March 2014), accessed November 8, 2018, https://tinyurl.com/yhcuyj6x.

8. Australian Royal Commission into Institutional Responses to Child Sexual Abuse (ARC). *Final Report*, vol. 3, 2017, 12, accessed October 30, 2018, https://tinyurl.com/yb89x6ar.

9. ARC, *Final Report*, 3:9.

10. Statistics Canada, *Family Violence in Canada: A Statistical Profile, 2015*, accessed November 9, 2018, https://tinyurl.com/yj5t4odn.

11. ARC, *Final Report*, 16, 586.

12. Robin F. Badgley et al., *Sexual Offences Against Children: Report of the Committee on Sexual Offences against Children and Youths [Canada]*, 1984. Doc no. J2-50/1984E-PDF, accessed December 3, 2018, https://tinyurl.com/yfrxrykr.

13. M. A. Ganje-Fling and P. McCarthy, "Impact of childhood sexual abuse on client spiritual development: Counseling implications," *Journal of Counseling & Development* 74, no. 3 (January–February

1996), 253–58.

14. Robert P. Allred, *Clergy Sexual Abuse,* PhD Dissertation (Ft. Lauderdale, FL: College of Psychology, Nova Southeastern University, 2015), 19, accessed November 9, 2018, https://tinyurl.com/yf42vhjt.

15. Thomas P. Doyle, *Abbreviated Bibliography of Selected Sources Related to Clergy Sexual Abuse, Ecclesiastical Politics, Theology and Church History*, 2013, accessed November 19, 2018, https://tinyurl.com/ygtgfvbv.

16. Donald F. Walker et al., "Changes in personal religion/spirituality during and after childhood abuse: A review and synthesis," *Psychological Trauma: Theory, Research, Practice, and Policy* 1, no. 2 (June 2009), 130–45, p. 130.

17. Karen J. Terry, lead researcher, *The Causes and Context of the Problem of Sexual Abuse of Minors by Catholic Priests and Deacons in the United States* (New York: John Jay College of Criminal Justice, 2011), 3, accessed October 28, 2018, https://tinyurl.com/69d8ofk.

18. Terry, *Causes and Context.* Also see therapist Thomas Plante's reflections on the differences between offenders in "Four Lessons Learned from Treating Catholic Priest Sex Offenders," *Pastoral Psychology* 64, no.3 (June 2015): 407–412, p. 409, https://scholarcommons.scu.edu/psych/75/.

19. US Department of Education, Office of the Under Secretary, *Educator sexual misconduct: A synthesis of existing literature*, by Charol Shakeshaft, doc # 2004-09 (Washington, DC, 2004), 26, accessed October 28, 2018, https://tinyurl.com/wwvs4pu.

20. Australian Royal Commission, vol. 16, p. 47.

21. John Kilpatrick et al., *Youth Victimization: Prevalence and Implications*, US National Department of Justice, National Institute of Justice, 2003, p. 5, accessed November 12, 2018, https://tinyurl.com/yj8llmfb.

22. US Department of Health and Human Services, Children's Bureau, *Child Maltreatment 2014*, accessed October 30, 2018, https://tinyurl.com/yzkkq3ka.

23. US Education, *Educator sexual misconduct*, 24–25.

24. Terry, *Causes and Context*, 8.

25. Plante, "Four Lessons." See also Cynthia Doxey, Larry Jensen, and Janet Jensen, "The Influence of Religion on Victims of Childhood Sexual Abuse," *International Journal for the Psychology of Religion* 7, no. 3 (1997), 179–86.

26. Andrew S. Denny et al., "Child Sexual Abuse in Protestant Christian Congregations: A Descriptive Analysis of Offense and Offender Characteristics," *Religions* 9, no. 1 (2018), 27ff., accessed October 16, 2018, https://tinyurl.com/yge2dkc8.

27. Joanna Scutts, "Britain's Boarding School Problem," *The New Republic*, September 14, 2018, https://tinyurl.com/yag2rkck.

28. Ian A. G. Barrie, *A Broken Trust*, in *Sex, Religion, Media*, ed. Dane S. Claussen (Lanham, MD: Rowman & Littlefield, 2002), 64–77, p. 70.

29. ARC, *Final Report*, 16: 447.

30. Joe Shute, "Why Tibetan Buddhism is facing up to its own abuse scandal," *The Telegraph*, September 8, 2018, https://tinyurl.com/y8ruw7hz.

31. Glenn L. Starks, *Sexual Misconduct and the Future of Large Mega-Churches: How Large Religious Organizations Go Astray* (Santa Barbara, CA: ABC-CLIO, LLC, 2013), 49.

32. Starks, *Mega-Churches*, 50.

33. ARC, *Final Report*, 16, 448.

34. Mary Finnigan, "The YouTube confessional sending shockwaves through the Buddhist world," *The Guardian*, March 9, 2012, https://tinyurl.com/y4332skl.

35. ARC, *Final Report*, 16, 45. As of December 2019 the Pope abolished Vatican secrecy rules for cases of sexual abuse. This allows the Catholic church to share documents and information with civil authorities (which, to a large extent, it already does in Canada and the US).

36. Tarico, "Protestant Clergy Sex Abuse."

37. Keenan, "CSA and the Catholic Church," 164.

38. Badgley, *Sexual Offenses Against Children in Canada*, 175.

39. M. Shields et al., "Is child sexual abuse declining in Canada? Results from nationally representative retrospective surveys," *Health Pro-*

motion and Chronic Disease Prevention in Canada 36, no. 11 (November 2016), 252–60, p. 252, https://tinyurl.com/ydruh6rt.

40. One good example: *Canadian Baptists of Western Canada*, "Preventing Abuse in the Church: Abuse Prevention Policies and Recommendations" (Calgary, AB, 2017).

5

Is It *Good* to Believe in God?
The Case for Healthy Religion

So far in this book, we have seen that belief in God—or better, "beliefs in gods," because people's convictions about divinity differ a great deal—sometimes leads to outcomes that vary from the sublime to the horrific. Given the repeated reality that in some individuals and communities religious beliefs take on nightmarish form, is belief in God worth the cost in human suffering?

Dan Barker, an atheist who writes for the *Freedom from Religion Foundation*, says no, at least as far as the god presented in the Bible is concerned:

> If Christianity were simply untrue, I would not be too concerned. Santa is untrue, but it is a harmless myth which people outgrow. But Christianity, besides being false, is also abhorrent. It amazes me that you claim to love the god of the bible, a hateful, arrogant, sexist, cruel being who can't tolerate criticism. I would not want to live in the same neighborhood with such a creature![1]

The late George Carlin, a well-known American stand-up comedian and countercultural critic, mocked what he saw as the prevailing view of God in American culture in a 1999 show at

the Beacon Theatre in New York (the text doesn't do him justice—you have to watch the video):

> Religion has actually convinced people that there's an invisible man
> living in the sky who watches everything you do, every minute of
> every day. And the invisible man has a special list of ten things he
> does not want you to do. And if you do any of these ten things, he
> has a special place, full of fire and smoke and burning and torture
> and anguish, where he will send you to live and suffer and burn and
> choke and scream and cry forever and ever 'til the end of time! . . .
> But He *loves* you. He loves you . . . and he needs *money!* He always
> needs money! He's all-powerful, all-perfect, all-knowing, and all-
> wise . . . somehow just can't handle money![2]

If, as Barker and Carlin insist, belief in God is not simply benign
but too often manifests as malignancy, perhaps it should be
actively discouraged. Perhaps we should be training our children
and grandchildren to discard belief in God the same way that our
ancestors turned their backs on witch-burnings, curses, and the
evil eye. Would it be better if the next generation had no faith in
the formal sense, if they evolved out of their "superstitions" into
more informed and less violent people?

Given the risks of abuse that we have already seen associated
with religious beliefs, is it best to help those beliefs die a natural—some would say long-overdue—death? Or would we lose
something essential to human well-being? To answer that question let's look more closely at what we mean by "religious
beliefs," especially belief in *God.* There are a couple of things that
should make us very cautious in what we say about God.

Our Gods Are "Homemade"

When I first visited India in 2003, I was greeted in the New
Delhi airport by the statue of a Hindu god with upraised arms
and a sign that said, "In India there are 36 crore [360 million]
gods—there should be one for you." Every Hindu village that I

visited on that trip had a "god-zoo" with statues of their gods behind bars (to prevent theft). Some had animal heads and/or bodies, multiple limbs, many faces. They presented as male, female, and nongendered, and were garbed as warriors, dancers, rulers, riders, scholars, and lovers. I was told that they were all limited expressions (or "avatars") of Brahman, the one absolute and eternal Creator. Each had its own personality and reflected some aspect of Brahman's creation.

I got the distinct impression that every village selected its own pantheon of gods according to local needs. For example, farmers living on unproductive land needed Parvati—a god of fertility; merchants looked to Ganesh for luck in their transactions and safety in their travels. Each community seemed to cobble together its unique form of religion out of a set of common Hindu elements, much (as we noted earlier) like a computer programmer would create an app, a "graphical user interface (GUI)," out of pre-developed code sets. Villagers would select the spiritual components that best related to their local needs and create a religious "app" (a "God-user-interface") that would enhance their common life.

Now I can immediately feel the resistance that committed believers might feel, especially in monotheistic faiths. Surely the god they worship can't be just a projection of their own needs (or ambitions) onto a big screen in the sky. How can we trust a straw god of our own making? And if we fashion our own gods, doesn't this simply make it easy for leaders with a self-centered agenda to present God as one who reinforces that leader's own power and prestige?

We will look at the question of how we can trust our religious apps in another chapter. But in answer to the latter question, *yes*, the fact that we create our images of God *does* make them vulnerable to being used for self-aggrandizement. In my book *Dis-*

covering the Other, I give an example from my visit to a Hindu village in Bengal:

> [The village] had experienced a great deal of distress due to the high number of children suffering from dysentery. Many babies died from it. Other children were left with serious disabilities. In the year before my arrival, an NGO had begun working with the mothers in that village. The women formed a self-help group that focused on sanitation, food safety, and access to potable water. As a result of their efforts, the childhood death rate dropped to a fraction of what it had been.
>
> I was curious about the role local religious leaders might have had in these dramatic changes and asked one of the women about it. She replied, "When we asked the priest why our children were dying, he told us it was the gods' punishment because we didn't come to worship. But now we know it was just bad hygiene. I think they wanted us to come and worship so that they will get more money for their livelihood."[3]

God-Talk Can Hurt or Heal

Clearly the benefits of a relationship with God depend heavily on how God is presented. And even then, the same presentation of God can have varying impacts, depending on the person and the situation. For example, a woman has been told that God is forgiving. Ordinarily she might see that as a good thing. But if she came to me after having been sexually assaulted and I said to her, "Your sins are forgiven," she would be shocked and hurt. The word of forgiveness (which Christian reformer Martin Luther regarded as the essence of the gospel—the Christian good news) might be life-giving in other circumstances, but at *this moment,* in *this particular woman's* life, it would imply that she was responsible for the assault against her. She needs to relate to God in a way that will counter the shame of violation she is feeling and give her some hope that her assailant will be brought to justice.

An ancient example: The biblical book of Revelation contains images of God consigning the "Anti-Christ" and "the Beast" (allusions to the oppressive power of the Roman Empire in the first century CE) to the fires of hell. For persecuted followers of Jesus who were hiding in the burial chambers under the city of Rome to avoid arrest and torture, "hell" was a hopeful image. It assured them that God would not be content to let oppressive regimes reign forever—that evil was unsustainable and that ultimately God would make things right.

Yet this same image of hell, in the hands of some twentieth-century Canadian residential schoolteachers, became a threat designed to ensure that "heathen" Indian boys and girls would remain compliant as their "savage" culture was stripped away.

Do you see how important the context is to the way we talk about God? Our religious apps are meant to serve particular people in particular contexts. So every religious group needs at least some of its respected members to be vigilantly critical of the way the group presents God to its members and wider community. They should ask, "Who is benefiting, right now, from this particular image of God? Who is suffering under it? How might a particular presentation of God affect the same people differently in different situations? What have been the real impacts, on the ground, of the way we have been imagining God?"

Certainly, there are signs that some people aren't happy with many of the old images. Some images exclude people from religious leadership on the basis of gender, race, and sexual orientation. Those are being challenged and starting to crumble. Many metaphors that traditionally imaged God as an old white man, as judge or king or policeman, are uncomfortable to many. They were used to justify the greater privileges given to dominant groups by implying that those groups are more *like* God, closer to God, and therefore deserve extra honor. That hierarchical view of human value is fading as the internet brings a greater global awareness of how much all humanity intrinsically has in common.

Today there are other images and metaphors of the Divine that are beginning to be used in worship settings. "Creator" is an ancient, but still valued image. I have seen people touched by depictions of God as "crucified woman," "weaver," "aboriginal warrior," "black nursing mother," "gushing fountain," "Latino construction worker," "playful Asian boy," "ancient redwood," "erupting volcano," "quirky inventor," "suffering planet," "middle eastern refugee," and many more. Such images are not common in public media, though there is a pervasive use of "the Universe" as a kind of neutral substitute for God.

One problem is that religious groups don't want to, or perhaps don't know how to, actively monitor whether the way they present God is a real benefit to people. What religious community do you know that regularly polls its members and visitors: "How were you affected by the way we talked about God at the mosque (church, temple) today?" It's much easier to pretend that the God-talk in our rituals, conversation, and holy books is good just because that's what we are used to or it's what our parents gave us. Or we may blithely assume that our way of talking about God is good because it is *universal*, that everyone of all times and places thinks and speaks the way we do about God.

It takes courage to ask: "Do the images of God our tradition has passed on to us still actually function to give life, to build community, *today?*" It's not automatically the case that old apps, religious or otherwise, continue forever to do what they were designed for (remember the almost disaster of Y2K?). Developing healthy God-talk takes open-hearted conversation with all those who use and hear it.

God-Talk Is Mostly about Us

God is an alien. Well, not so much *an* alien, as just completely *alien to us*—and everything we know. We are creatures, God is not. That is the problem with talking about God. All that we can experience directly are *created* things—people, plants, stars, fridges, dirt, dogs, and so on. We have no words or concepts for that which is entirely outside our experience. As a result, talking theology (as I've done for a living) is like fish trying to describe what it's like to be an astronaut. Mostly nonsense, really.

One of my children drew attention to the problem. Like all children, mine asked a lot of "Why?" questions when they were young (especially at bedtime). I think they were genuinely curious, but they also wanted to stay up a bit later and loved to torture their much-educated pastor-theologian father, who was supposed to know it all but obviously didn't.

At one such bedtime, our four-year-old son finished his prayers and then (ironically) he looked me in the eye and said very solemnly, "Dad, I don't think I can believe in God anymore." "Why?" I asked. "Because I can't understand how God couldn't have a beginning," he said. It floored me. All I could say was, "Yeah, that's a tough one for me too. Everything I know has a beginning. I guess God is completely different from everything else."

Our God-talk tries to point at something (which is clearly not some "thing"—you see the problem already) that is truly outside of us, beyond. And not *beyond*, the way stars or other galaxies or quarks are beyond us. God is beyond anything we could *ever* discover with our telescopes or spaceships or the Large Hadron Collider at CERN. In fact, God doesn't *exist*. So, one can't even properly say God "is." Rather, God *makes existence possible*. As Hebrew scholar Michael Heiser notes, the name given to God in the Jewish Torah—YHWH—is best translated "I *is*"—that is, "*I cause [things] to be.*"[4]

When we face that Divine differentness straight on, as my son did that night, we can almost feel repelled. You know how you have felt when you have encountered a person who was really different from you in skin or hair color, with strange tats, wearing camo pants or an Armani suit, shouting crazy slogans with beery breath, or whatever. You want to pull back, draw away. Well, becoming aware of the unimaginably greater "alienness" of God can be, to say the least, alienating.

Some people retreat from it into a kind of shrunken secularism, ignoring the world of spirit to focus on accumulating stuff, staying entertained, having fun, keeping the happy brain chemicals humming.

Others react with a thoughtful agnosticism. There is a long tradition of "apophasis" that says, if we can't say anything sensible about God, we shouldn't say anything about God at all. A slightly less severe version is that of "negative theology," which doesn't try to say what God *is* but affirms what God is *not* (e.g., "not limited—by time, space, power," "not evil," "not mortal," and so on). And some, of course, react by adopting a strong "anti-God" position like atheists such as Christopher Hitchens or Richard Dawkins.

True atheists (there are fewer than one might think) do not simply take potshots at popular caricatures of God that no thoughtful believer would really trust or endorse anyway. There are plenty of silly, idolatrous images constantly popping up in pulpits, casual conversation, and the media. Most are a riff on the superhero motif—as if God were an extremely large, well-muscled (sometimes bearded) Thor. They're easy to ridicule. But people of genuine faith will be as critical of such portrayals of God as atheists are.

Perhaps the most genuine atheist is one like my son who (for a brief while anyway) saw how *un*like, how utterly beyond, how incomprehensible a real Creator must be—and shuddered. I suspect it is beyond our human capacity to squarely face that great Unknown Other.

Ambushed by God

I don't think we are left simply with a choice between bleak silence—staring into the face of Infinite Mystery—or worshipping a stuffed god that we've dressed in our favorite clothes and propped up front in our churches. Because there are hints that while *our* quest to contact God may be futile, *God has made contact with us.* In an unbroken line back to the most ancient of human cultures, people have told stories not of *discovering* God, or *figuring out* who God is, but of being in some way *addressed by* Someone/Thing deeper, higher, completely outside themselves.

When Irish professor of English and confirmed atheist C. S. Lewis admitted to himself at the age of thirty-one that he probably should take God into account, he described himself as "the most dejected and reluctant convert in all England . . . brought in kicking, struggling, resentful, and darting his eyes in every direction for a chance of escape." What changed his mind (in fact his fundamental orientation to life)? He says it was a recurrent experience of being "surprised by joy":

> In a sense the central story of my life is about nothing else. . . . The quality common to the three experiences . . . is that of an unsatisfied desire which is itself more desirable than any other satisfaction. I call it Joy, which is here a technical term and must be sharply distinguished both from Happiness and Pleasure. Joy (in my sense) has indeed one characteristic, and one only, in common with them; the fact that anyone who has experienced it will want it again. . . . I doubt whether anyone who has tasted it would ever, if both were in his power, exchange it for all the pleasures in the world.[5]

Lewis's experience is not uncommon. Sometimes we are simply caught off-guard by something outside ourselves. I remember seeing a Christian Passion play at a conference in Regina, Saskatchewan. I was watching a bit half-heartedly, as I'd seen many such plays before. But at the scene where Jesus asks Peter, "Do you love me?" I suddenly felt an enormous upwelling inside, as though a dam broke. And I began to cry. A sobbing, snotty cry! I was pretty embarrassed (being a Spock-type guy surrounded by colleagues), but I couldn't stem the flow. I had to leave the auditorium, stumbled to my room, and literally wept on and off for a couple of hours. The tears simply wouldn't stop. They were strange tears—not of sadness, relief, loss, or the many other things people normally cry over. What I felt was an intense, overwhelming longing, as though I was completely loved, and I desperately desired, but couldn't quite reach, the Lover. When the waterworks finally ended, I felt . . . the best I can describe it is something like a child in the womb who has just become vividly aware of their mother.

In trying to talk about such experiences, we are a bit like a box turtle crossing a road. A car comes along and stops. A man gets out, picks up the turtle, and puts her in the car. All of a sudden, the turtle's life is turned upside down—literally. The man takes her to his house, introduces her to his friends, smuggles her into a movie theater, gives her a taste of popcorn and coke, and then returns her to the side of the road where he found her. What would the turtle tell her friends? She knows nothing about humans and their world. The most she can do is describe how the encounter with that human affected her: "I was frightened. I felt out of control. I was lifted up. I felt inspected but wasn't harmed. It was awesome—but I don't really know what It was."

When two of Jesus's disciples met Jesus on the road to Emmaus after his resurrection and then ate with him (Luke 24:13–35), that's about all they could say, too. Their witness to the encounter was not an analysis of the once-dead, now-living Jesus. It was simply a report of what that meeting had done to them: "Our hearts burned within us!" (v. 32).

Perhaps faith, at its barest, is not much more or less than this—not clinging to particular ideas ("beliefs") about Divine Being(s) or keeping codes of conduct to avoid punishment and get a reward after death, but simply being grasped for a moment by Something far beyond ourselves yet intimately connected to our deepest being, feeling a *fire* kindled inside.

If so, then in one sense it doesn't matter what judgment we render in our cost-benefit analysis of belief in God. Apparently, faith (or "joy," to use Lewis's term) can ambush anyone, including those who are looking for it, those who've rejected it, and even those who couldn't care less. And all seem to be changed by the experience. Faith then is probably best described not as a set of *ideas* about God, but as a *relationship* God develops with us. As Paul writes in his letter to the Christians at Ephesus, faith is a *gift*. Maybe so.

What Gifts Do Religious Organizations Bring to Their Communities?

Religion, however, is a different matter. Religion, as I keep repeating, is a human social construction, an "app" people design to interpret, or sustain, reproduce, and sometimes attempt to control the "God-surprise." Assuming one's religious community has an app that is reasonably life-giving to its members, what difference does it make to the community around it? What benefits does religion provide to society that might offset its potential harms?

The "rite" stuff for life's critical passages

Alain de Botton is an atheist who thinks that the social structures of religion are actually necessary to healthy human life. In his book *Religion for Atheists: A Non-believer's Guide to the Uses of Religion*, de Botton argues that religions are not primarily a set of claims about a Divine being but are essentially "machines for living." In an interview with De Botton by Sean Illing (titled "Religion without God: Alain de Botton on 'atheism 2.0'"), De Botton says:

> [Religions] aim to guide you from birth to death and to teach you a whole range of things: to create a community, to create codes of behavior, to generate aesthetic experiences. . . . They are trying to locate the tenets of a good life, of a wise life, of a kind life . . . to provide us with tools for how to keep being the best version of ourselves.[6]

The problem, it seems, is that apart from some elements of children's education, there are not many alternative institutions that offer the comprehensive set of rituals, social support, art, stories, and music that religions provide to help build that good life and good community. *Guardian* columnist and atheist Suzanne Moore describes her personal struggle to find meaningful, sensual, nonreligious rites for her family life. In an online article entitled "Why non-believers need rituals too," she notes after several so-so experiments that "it is very hard to do this without borrowing from traditional [religious] symbols."[7]

Working with smaller communities around the world, I have seen over and over how worship centers have led their communities to celebrate, grieve, and grow through critical passages and the annual rhythms of life. They provide rituals that bind people together and lay out their lives before the cosmos in powerful ancient imagery.

Companionship in suffering

Faith communities also provide accompanists—not musicians (though that too!) but folks who will walk with the injured and bewildered through the endless maze of bureaucratic red tape that has become our institutional life in the West. (Our congregation has a group of such trained accompanists called "Stephen Ministers.")

An unusual example: one woman that I visited in hospital was deeply depressed over her taxes—not because she couldn't pay them, but because she couldn't figure them out! The tax documents were so complex she finally had to take them to a tax specialist. But the specialist made a grievous error. The woman, who was extremely conscientious, found herself unable to stay inside the law: she couldn't do her own taxes accurately and couldn't trust anyone else to do them either. The anxiety led to a mental breakdown. Our church walked beside her to help find a reliable accountant and oversee their work. In the end, she received an all-clear from Revenue Canada and the hospital, and she was able to resume normal life.

A talking place to process life's key questions

The internet was supposed to be the great venue for open conversation. But as many analysts have noted, social media have a powerful tendency to support confirmation bias. Social media encourage people to pass on more and more material that confirms what they already think, forming tightly closed idea tribes.[8] Faith communities, in contrast, often include a wider cross-section of local society in their membership. So, folks who wouldn't "friend" each other on Facebook end up sitting side-by-side in the pew or face-to-face at the church potluck.

In an era when the United States, and Canada to some extent, seem to be increasingly polarized, the bravest religious communities are bringing people together across political, racial, and class divides to talk about the stuff that matters most in their lives and their country. They help to nurture critical thinking about ethical matters and build understanding between people who are divided by stereotypes.

In *Discovering the Other*, I discuss the community benefits I've just mentioned, and others, in greater detail.[9] To those I'll add three more:

Disproportionate gifts of money and volunteer time

First, and very practically, active churchgoers punch far above their weight in donating time and money to community needs. According to the Canadian Centre for Philanthropy, weekly worship attenders in Canada who volunteer make up 9 percent of all Canadians, but they account for *39 percent* of all hours volunteered.[10]

Statistics Canada's 2013 study of Canadian charitable giving reveals that, on average, Canadians who attend church regularly give about four times as much to charities as those who never attend. The reason for their generosity: "they felt compassion towards people in need" (91 percent); "helping a cause in which they personally believed" (88 percent); and "wanting to make a contribution to their community" (82 percent).[11]

Similar statistics for giving apply to people in the United States. According to the Philanthropy Roundtable, Americans give substantially more to charities generally than other nations (twice as much as Canadians, ten times as much as Europeans)—about $400 billion each year. Who are those givers? Not foundations and corporations, which together donate less than a fifth of that total. American givers, by and large, are *individuals* who are *reli-*

gious, *conservative*, and *rural* (which may not fit everyone's image of big donors).[12] They give far more than others, not just to their own churches, but to *all kinds of charities*.[13]

It is the highly churched population of America, especially rural and small-town America, that funds the great life-giving organizations of the country—everything from schools and scholarships to sports clubs, health research, international relief agencies, Audubon societies, theatre and arts groups, human rights advocates, and quilting and woodworking guilds. Imagine what we would lose without them!

Excellent health care institutions

Second, and critical to the longer lives we now enjoy, religions have been instrumental in establishing good health care. It is striking that the origin stories of many religious groups center around health:

- Dietary laws in Judaism and Islam appear to have been formulated largely to reduce the danger of food-borne diseases.

- In Christianity, the Greek word often translated "to save" (*soidzo*) is better rendered "to heal." Jesus's ministry begins with the healing of Peter's mother-in-law and ends with his restoring the ear of one who had come to arrest him (Peter had cut it off trying to defend Jesus).

- The Buddha is also spoken of as a "Great Physician" because of his deep concern for people's suffering and his steady work to help them find relief.

- And Islam, like Judaism, has always had at its core a sense of *salaam* (*shalom* in Hebrew). *Shalom/salaam* is often translated "peace" in English, but this is not peace as Americans and Canadians use the term—as an absence of war, or an untroubled spirit. Shalom/salaam is *wholeness, flourishing*, what we think of as "health."

For centuries churches, mosques, synagogues, and temples have worked tirelessly to bring health care to their communities. Over the last millennium, as fledgling nations in the West developed their infrastructure, faith-based groups have been heavily represented in the establishment of hospitals, hospices, nursing orders, long-term care, and other healing ministries. In fact, in the early American colonies, many of the clergy were also physicians.

In Western nations most faith-based healing institutions eventually get turned over to civil authorities. And for a while in North America this led many to assume that religion would fade out of the health care picture. But recently there has been a growing awareness of a strong correlation between active participation in religious groups and better health outcomes.[14] In a 2012 article, Duke University faculty member and psychiatrist Harold Koenig documents a dramatic upswing since 2000 in research studies exploring that connection.[15] These studies show that faith-based groups support the health of their members in many important ways. For example, religious organizations:

- Help people cope better with physical and mental illness by nurturing positive emotions such as gratitude, self-esteem, hope, kindness, and forgiveness.

- Reduce stress responses by assuring people that no matter what happens, their lives are in the hands of a God who loves them, listens to their prayers, and will help them through their illness or disability.

- Promote a way of life that generally includes fewer risk factors to health—for example moderate or no use of alcohol and recreational drugs, fidelity in marriage, and care for children and the elderly. And a 2007 study by sociologist Christopher Ellison found "religious involvement, specifically church attendance, *protects against domestic violence,* and this protective effect is stronger for African American men and women and for Hispanic men, groups that, for a variety of reasons, experience elevated risk for this type of violence."[16]

- Encourage the ill to seek medical help and provide practical assistance in navigating the often-torturous bureaucracy that dispenses that help. In fact, in rural communities where medical facilities are rare or distant, it is most often faith communities that mobilize transportation, emergency support for the patient's family, and prayer networks, and even provide first aid.

- Emphasize the ongoing, intrinsic value of people who may feel shamed, even worthless because of their illness or disability.

- Organize visitation of the sick and provide emotional support that reduces the incidence of depression, anxiety, substance abuse, and suicide. This positive attention is such a powerful antidote to mental illness—and so significant in recovery from other illnesses—that doctors in the UK can now routinely prescribe "social remedies" or "community referrals" for their patients (more about this below).

- Provide ethical assistance in making decisions about health matters such as abortion, physician-assisted death, and do-not-resuscitate orders. Authoritarian religious groups are likely to give a pronouncement on these matters, and that isn't always helpful. But more democratically structured churches frequently engage their members in open, critical reflection on difficult ethical questions related to health.

Of course, some religious groups attend to health matters better than others. Some are so exclusively concerned about people's *spiritual* well-being, or their health *after death*, that they neglect the physical life now.

And some religious groups actively damage members' health by treating illness as a sign of God's disfavor, or as an attack by demonic powers. Such assumptions have ancient roots. One can see them, for example, in the Jewish scriptures, when Job's friends point to Job's illness and the disasters that befell his family as a sign that Job had angered God. (He hadn't, it turns out.) And in the Christian gospels Jesus often heals people who appear to be mentally ill but are shunned because they are assumed to be "demon-possessed."

When religious groups take illness as a sign of moral evil (a sort of false "karmic" justice), members may hide symptoms of illness or avoid going to doctors, so they don't jeopardize their "righteous" standing in the group.

I saw something of the latter when a young fellow (I'll call him Fred) came to visit me. I knew Fred was very short-sighted, but to my surprise, when I opened the door, he wasn't wearing glasses. "Did you get contacts?" I asked. "No," Fred replied, "I've been healed." Then he proceeded to feel his way into the room, stepping carefully with his arms out to avoid bumping into things. "It doesn't look like you can see any better than before," I said. "Oh yes," Fred insisted, "my church prayed for me, and I was healed. I know I've still got some symptoms, but they said if I just had *faith*, the symptoms would disappear." Well, maybe they would, as long as Fred didn't fall down the stairs and break his neck first!

But these are aberrations for the most part. In my experience there is a deep vein of *grace* in the best religious traditions, a sense that every life is held in the hands of a compassionate God who responds to suffering and cares for sufferers.

An eye for those who fall through the cracks

Finally, religious groups are often good at spotting and catching those who fall through the cracks in social and economic systems. New faith-based NGOs are constantly springing up to care for untended human needs. This eye for the forgotten may have its roots in the fact that new religions almost always form at the *edges* of an established religion. It's not usually those at the center—priests and religious managers—who are hungry for change, because they're invested in the status quo. They've got little to gain by making waves. So, it is the mavericks, the exiles, the spiritually disturbed or little-noticed who tend to be the sparkplugs for novel religious expression.

Perhaps it is because of their own "edgy" history that religions develop an eye for those on the margins of society, those who fall through the gaps in government safety nets and don't have their own social net to catch them. They know what it means to be loved by a "God of the gaps."

I experienced this in my work with "Micah"—an ecumenical nonprofit in Saskatoon that works with offenders. The organization developed when various churches in our city noted that there were some not-so-grand canyons in the way that Canada deals with its lawbreakers. First of all, a large majority of offenders have some form of mental illness or emotional scars from childhood mistreatment. But our system tends to "warehouse" offenders rather than treat, retrain, or rehabilitate them.

Second, during the time offenders spend in prison, their families on the outside often distance themselves. Other inmates, who are not very good role models, take the family's place. When offenders are eventually released, they are relatively unemployable and often have only their old prison buddies to turn to, or in the case of sexual offenders, no one.

Third, it is not then surprising that people who are blocked from normal avenues for making a living and have very little social support apart from other ex-cons, are likely to turn to crime again to meet their needs. So, we set up our prisoners to re-offend, and in the process, create more victims and more cost to society.

The church groups that formed Micah saw that our justice system can be, in some ways, a school for crime. Their conviction was that both offenders and the community they've hurt are loved by God. And yet, they saw that the real needs of both are largely being ignored. Criminals are being punished, but in the end, society can actually be more endangered and damaged as a result.

So Micah developed three ministries to help fill that gap: (1) they train volunteers to build long-term mentoring relationships with prisoners; (2) they develop programs to help released offenders find jobs and good friends; and (3) they create "Circles of Support and Accountability" (COSAs) to help released sex offenders maintain a safe and healthy lifestyle.

At coffee after a COSA meeting, one of these former sex offenders said to me, "When I'm really down I sometimes think about re-offending, but then I remember how much this group cares about me, how hard they have worked to help me stay clean, and I put those bad thoughts away, because I would never want to jeopardize my relationship with them." Government studies of COSA effectiveness show that their participants have a *much* lower incidence of re-offending than a matching group of non-COSA offenders (83 percent reduction for sexual crimes and 73 percent reduction in all types of violent offenses).[17]

I have also participated with church groups in starting other efforts similar to Micah, including a women's shelter, a chapter of Habitat for Humanity, and CiRCLe M—an organization that helps rural churches build healthier rural communities.[18] All were created because people were falling through the cracks of government programs.

Recently Britain recognized the essential role of religious and other community organizations in gap-filling when it gave its physicians the right to prescribe "social remedies." Its website describes the inherent irony:

> Those who find themselves excluded from society, discriminated against, or lacking power and control because of living in extreme poverty, can be the least likely to access and benefit from services—despite often having the worst health. Adopting more community-centered practice can help provide more appropriate and effective ways of engaging people and improving their health and wellbeing.[19]

So then, to conclude this chapter we ask again: Faith . . . is it worth it? I think we've seen that this question may be moot. Faith itself isn't always something we seek or choose. More often faith (God) finds us. But organized religion is another matter. Religions can be assessed, joined, dismissed. I've tried to look at both their costs and benefits, but you can see that I've thrown in my cap with those who are convinced that *good* religion (and there's lots of it out there) is worth it. What do you think?

Explore!

1. Go online to Google Maps. Search for "religious organizations" in your town or neighborhood. Click on a couple of their websites, and see what kinds of ministry they are involved in. Are they helping people who are "falling through the cracks"? Are they hosting any use-

ful conversations? What kinds of connections or part-
nerships do they seem to have with the community?

2. Have you benefited directly from a religious organization (worship center or nonprofit) that helped you
in a time of need? If so, what was the experience like
for you? Did the organization, or the folks you worked
with directly, connect their faith explicitly to the work
they were doing? If so, in what way?

3. Discuss with a friend: What's the result of your personal
cost-benefit analysis so far (there's more to come in the
book of course)? How are you leaning at this point?
Does religion seem to be worth it or should we be trying to steer the next generation away from it?

Notes

1. Dan Barker, "Dear Believer," *Freedom from Religion Foundation*,
accessed December 30, 2018, https://tinyurl.com/yew553ce.

2. George Carlin, "You Are All Diseased," comedy show, New York:
Beacon Theatre, February 6, 1999, https://tinyurl.com/yjxh6f3p.
See video at time stamp 52:25.

3. Harder, *Discovering the Other*, 37–38.

4. Michael Heiser, "YHWH," online article, accessed November 13,
2019 at https://tinyurl.com/s8bpntq.

5. C. S. Lewis, *Surprised by Joy: The Shape of My Early Life*, p. 24.
First published in 1955 by Geoffrey Bles (UK) and Harcourt Brace
(US), now public domain in Canada, accessed March 14, 2019,
https://tinyurl.com/yeq6dvl6.

6. Alain de Botton, *Religion for Atheists: A Non-believer's Guide to the
Uses of Religion* (Toronto: Penguin Random House Canada, 2013).
See also De Botton's interview with Sean Illing, accessed March
13, 2019, https://tinyurl.com/ydxyv27y.

7. Suzanne Moore, "Why non-believers need rituals too," *The

Guardian, December 27, 2013, https://tinyurl.com/yeuqgjvd.

8. The September 2019 issue of *Scientific American* is titled "Truth, Lies and Uncertainty" and has several good articles on the ways in which open-minded social conversation is being inhibited.

9. Harder, *Discovering the Other*, previously cited, 49-72.

10. Kurt Bowen, "Religion, Participation and Charitable Giving" (Toronto: Canadian Centre for Philanthropy, 1999), 12.

11. Statistics Canada, "Spotlight on Canadians: Results from the General Social Survey Charitable Giving by Individuals," by Martin Turcotte, 2015, https://tinyurl.com/yeu65gnn.

12. See Karl Zinsmeister, "Who Gives Most to Charity?" *Philanthropy Roundtable: The Almanac*, accessed April 24, 2019, https://tinyurl.com/yg5peyxo.

13. *Giving USA*, "Giving USA Special Report on Giving to Religion," report summary, October 24, 2017, https://tinyurl.com/yf78kgg3.

14. See for example Lynda Powell et al., "Religion and Spirituality: Linkages to Physical Health," *American Psychologist* 58, no. 1 (February 2003), 36–52.

15. Harold Koenig, "Religion, Spirituality, and Health: The Research and Clinical Implications," *ISRN Psychiatry*, 2012: 1–33, accessed September 21, 2019, https://tinyurl.com/yh52otv9. Two more excellent references for the connection between religion and health: Harold Koenig et al., *Handbook of Religion and Health*, 2nd ed. (New York: Oxford University Press, 2012); and Ellen L. Idler, ed., *Religion as a Social Determinant of Public Health* (New York: Oxford University Press, 2014).

16. Christopher Ellison, "Race/Ethnicity, Religious Involvement, and Domestic Violence," in *Violence Against Women* 13, no. 11 (2007), 1094–1112, https://www.ncbi.nlm.nih.gov/pubmed/17951587.

17. Robin Wilson, Franca Cortoni, and Andrew McWhinnie, "Circles of Support & Accountability: A Canadian National Replication of Outcome Findings," *Sexual Abuse: A Journal of Research and Treatment* 21, no. 4 (2009), 412–30, https://doi.org/10.1177/1079063209347724.

18. *Camrose Women's Shelter*, https://camrosewomenshelter.org/; *Habitat for Humanity Camrose*, https://habitatcamrose.com/; *Centre for*

Rural Community Leadership and Ministry ("CiRCLe M"), http://www.circle-m.ca.

19. *Public Health England*, "Social Prescribing: Applying All Our Health," updated June 17, 2019, https://tinyurl.com/yz3tgmtx.

6

Are Faith and Science Compatible?

Even if religion, in its healthy forms, offers some things that are valuable to human well-being, there are still a couple of hard questions that thoughtful people stumble over. The first, which we will look at in this chapter, is whether religion is compatible with a worldview shaped by twenty-first century science. The second is the question of suffering, which we will tackle in the next chapter.

Signs of Mutual Distrust

I've recently had two young people I care for express intense anxiety about the future of our planet. One said, "I'm afraid this will be the last time we have a year ending in the 'teens'"—in other words, "I'm afraid there won't be a habitable earth, or at least a human race, a century from now." They're worried about the accelerating pace of climate change, extinction of species, and the poisoning of land, air, and water.

While Centennials (those born after 2000) may have deep concerns about what scientists are telling them, some (certainly not all) religious communities are ignoring those warnings. There are many reasons for this. For example, as we shall see in the final chapter, some religious traditions teach that this world is disposable; it's ultimately going to be trashed in favor of a "new heaven and earth," so why worry about it. But a common contributing factor is a simple distrust of science. In part that may be due to the extraordinary success of modern science and the accelerating pace of new discoveries. Science has become very complex so quickly that scientific applications can seem like magic and its practitioners like wizards. It's hard to trust what we don't understand.

But it is also true that in the last century or so, many religious leaders in the United States and Canada have taught, implicitly or explicitly, that science is *antagonistic* to the Bible and other sacred scriptures, and therefore antagonistic to faith. They say you can accept the sacred story *or* the scientific story but *not both*. People of faith who pay too much attention to science are assumed to be in danger of putting their faith in science "magicians" rather than in God. As a result, they stand to lose the respect of their faith community. Those are big stakes, so it's not hard to see why some religious folks might shy away from scientific pronouncements about global warming or evolution.

It turns out that scientists are pretty skeptical about religion too. A Pew Research Center study of Americans in 2009 found that only about half as many scientists believe in God or a higher power as does the general population.[1] Smaller Canadian studies indicate even less belief among scientists. And in the Pew study, biologists were least likely to believe; 80 percent identified themselves as atheists. I've seen it myself. I've been involved with academia for almost sixty years. Many scientists I've met confess that they feel a lot of pressure from their peers to ignore, reject, or stay silent about religious commitments.

So . . . here we have a suffering planet, suffering to a great degree at the hands of humans, we are told. But two groups of humans who could really help to change that are at loggerheads with each other: the religious folks who tend the human conscience and help us see the value of God's creation . . . and the scientists who monitor the health of the earth. No wonder Centennials are frightened when it looks like their parents are so paralyzed by prejudice that they can't act to protect their children's future!

A Story of Mutual Enrichment

I don't think the breach is impossible to bridge. I had a rather remarkable conversation with a biologist—a weed scientist—at a rural ministry conference in Ontario one year. He had been brought in to speak about the native plant ecology of agricultural communities (i.e., "weeds"). But he clearly wasn't too comfortable in a Christian setting. During the worship services he sat at the back, silent, not participating.

At one point in the conference, both he and I ended up alone in a workshop—even the leader didn't show—so we started talking. And, because it was the conference theme, we got onto the subject of creation. He said he wasn't sure how all this talk about God related to his work with weeds. But he shared some of the marvels that he has seen working with plants at a microscopic level.

I was touched by his passion for those native plants. I said that I see his "weeds" as a wonderful part of a great universe story in which Love drew out of darkness an explosion of galaxies that, over eons of time, through the interplay of gravity and other forces, has resulted in the life forms he studies. I told him I believe that marvelous Love is God, working to bring ever greater beauty and complexity into being. I pointed out how, in spite of entropy, *life* has entered the universe and brought into being *conscious* life, and *self-conscious* life, and even *God-conscious* life. "So," I offered, "when you study a plant, you are looking at a masterpiece that has taken God almost 14 billion years to create."

Anyway, we talked in that vein for a while. He noted how the death of some species leads to the emergence of new forms of life; I noticed that the same thing happens in Jesus's death and resurrection. And we speculated about what might lie ahead for this amazing universe of ours.

Later that morning, the scientist stood up to give his keynote address. He was a little way into it when he suddenly stopped and said, "I have to tell you that something has happened to me this morning. I spend my days studying very small things—the roots of a dandelion, plant enzymes. Sometimes it seems like a tedious exercise in filtration and dissection. But in a conversation today, I realized that my work is part of a larger story, a universal story, about life, and love and maybe even God. I have to say, it makes all that I'm doing seem worthwhile. It gives me hope. You are so lucky to know that story—because the people I work with mostly don't." And then he choked up . . . and sat down.

A scientist and a theologian exchanged gifts that morning. I offered the scientist a frame in which to view his work—I hope one that enhanced his wonder and hope and sense of meaning in what he is doing. He gave me a look inside the astonishing world hidden in the cells of native prairie plants.

For me the encounter was a precious gift, not least because in university I was a physics student and have been an avid science reader ever since. With coffee and *Scientific American* in hand, I pester my wife constantly over breakfast with the startling news that a teaspoon scoop of a neutron star would weigh 10 million tons—or that gene gun therapy may one day cure a genetic disease our family has been plagued with.

I love science because it reveals the astonishing beauty and complexity of creation as well as its hidden dangers and drama. Like the best of music critics, science traces the intricate paths of movement and color, sound and silence, that make up the universe symphony. In the process, science tunes my ears to the "music of the spheres," draws me into the medley of praise that the Hebrew psalmist described: "The heavens declare the glory of God; the sky displays the Creator's handiwork. Day after day it speaks out; night after night it reveals God's greatness" (Ps 19:1).

Working Together

Historically (in spite of some well-known exceptions) religion supported scientific enquiry. Faith has always been convinced that creation is not a chaos soup but is governed by laws that can be discovered by careful inquiry. So, in the ninth to fifteenth centuries, Muslim caliphates in the Middle East were fervent patrons of the maths, astronomy, medicine, and other sciences, enabling the Islamic world to leap ahead of Europe in its scientific knowledge during that period. In India, from the sixth century BCE, Hindu understandings of Brahman as manifest in natural phenomena spurred investigation of astronomy, linguistics, and mathematics. Christian thinkers from Augustine (fourth century) on argued that God was revealed in the "book of nature" and that nature therefore deserved close attention.[2]

These days, a number of people are trying to bridge the science-faith divide. Here are just a few examples: geneticist Francis Collins, director of the Human Genome Project;[3] Evangelical Christian climatologist Katharine Hayhoe;[4] Muslim physicist Nidhal Guessoum;[5] Catholic theologian John Haught;[6] Hindu quantum physicist Mani Lal Bhaumik;[7] neuroscientist and Tibetan Buddhist monk Alan Wallace;[8] and (carrying over from the bridge-builders of the twentieth century) Anglican priest and physicist John Polkinghorne.[9]

Let's look at some of the benefits of strengthening that connection.

Science helps religion "take out the trash"

Science helps clear away some of religion's least useful understandings of humanity, the world, and God. We will look at some of these in more detail further on. Briefly, science pokes a pin in human pride, deflating the tendency to see ourselves at the center of creation, as its saving angels or destructive demons, and the only significant object of God's interest and love. By showing us the vast scales of the universe (smaller and larger than we are), it helps us find a humbler, more appropriate place in the universe. As theologian Jürgen Moltmann reminds us, that song of praise to the Creator I just mentioned "was sung *before* the appearance of human beings, is sung *outside* the sphere of human beings and will be sung even *after* human beings have—perhaps—disappeared from this planet."[10]

In a related vein, science also counters religious folks' tendency to be self-focused, obsessed with our own purity or ultimate happiness but blithely unaware of how we impact the world. We tend to relegate "nature" to the background; we see it as our "environment"—the furniture in the room that God built for us. But we can be blithely unaware of the real effect we have on it. Science counters that narcissistic ignorance by showing us the deep continuity and connectedness of all things, from the quantum to the intergalactic (or multiverse?) levels. It teaches us that while we are not the center; we do affect and are affected by the whole. In the process we come to realize that we don't just live *on* the Land, we *are* the Land, and the Land lives in us.

Third, science helps us get rid of our concept of God as a Divine engineer who built this world, then left it largely to itself, popping in ("Deus ex Machina") only to fix the occasional problem that we bring to God in prayer. As science provides explanations for what were once mysteries, the "gaps" where such a God can act or be revealed get smaller and smaller. Science then leaves religion with only two choices: Either the universe is entirely a random accident and has no Creator, or else there is a Creator who is intimately involved with every atom and cell in the universe—a living, immanent, constantly creating God (which, in Christian terms is a reasonable version of the way the Bible as a whole presents God).

Finally, science helps religion distinguish between baseless convictions and indirect evidence. Religions sometimes seem to advocate "blind" faith. Christian tradition, for example, has often pointed to Jesus's encounter with his follower Thomas after Jesus's resurrection. Like a good scientist, Thomas asks for evidence that this is indeed Jesus ("until I put my finger into mark of the nails and place my hand in the wound in his side, I will not believe," John 20:25). But Jesus says, "Blessed are those who have *not* seen and yet believe" (v. 29). It might seem that Jesus is endorsing religious gullibility. But in fact, the author of John's gospel goes on to point out that there were a great number of witnesses to Jesus's life and work (many not even mentioned in his writing—v. 30). Essentially, he is saying that while the faith of those who come after Thomas cannot be directly based on a physical encounter with Jesus, it can still be based on reliable *evidence* from observers.

Scientists verify the value of indirect evidence for things that we cannot personally observe. For example, quarks, electrons, Higgs bosons, and other atomic building blocks cannot be directly seen by scientists, but their *effects* can be traced (in the Hadron Collider for example). And those concepts have turned out to be very useful, enabling engineers to make all kinds of amazing things from smart phones to x-ray machines.

Just as science sees real, if indirect, evidence of electrons in light bulbs and lightning, so people of faith have seen real, if indirect, evidence of God's presence in Muhammad's reception of the Qur'an, the Hebrews' exodus from Egypt, the person of Jesus Christ, and the experiences of their own lives.

Science helps religion see the Creator's creativity in creation

Science has helped us map the extraordinary unfolding of the universe and our own planet—from a singularity (I like the ancient religious term "cosmic egg," popularized by Belgian priest Georges Lemaître in the 1920s) to the unimaginably complex structure we know today. Most of this unfolding appears to have a kind of experimental quality—as if it were the work of a mixed-media artist like Pablo Picasso, who believed art can be made out of any assortment of things.

For example, in the Rocky Mountains just west of my birthplace (Calgary, Alberta), there is an extraordinary fossil bed called the Burgess Shale. It is a stunning example of the enormous diversity of life-forms that emerged during the Cambrian Explosion about half a billion years ago, when life on earth suddenly morphed from single-celled organisms into a wild (often bizarre) mélange of multicellular creatures. One of them is *Marrella splendens*, a lace crab with twenty-six pairs of legs that breathed by "kicking" its legs (there is a gill on each leg). Another —*Opabinia*—has five eyes on stubby stalks, a flat head, and a long vacuum cleaner hose for a nose. The fossils in the Burgess Shale have a quirky quality about them—as if almost every conceivable arrangement of legs, eyes, noses, and bodies was being tried out. As one would expect, many of the life forms do not appear to have lasted. However, lots of those that were well adapted to their environment, and sustainable, hung on for the long term.

In bringing earth's living history to light, scientists have helped us see that nature does not have rigid, eternal, unchanging structures. As we will see, there do not appear to be unalterable divinely designed "orders of creation." If life then isn't confined to a few rigid, unbreachable categories, religions should take that into consideration as they help their people face ethical challenges. Finding what is "good" for now is not about discovering what has always been "natural."

In normalizing such diversity, science also helps free us from our fear of the new. It lets us celebrate, rather than try to eradicate, the kaleidoscope of kin with which we share this planet: the clownfish and West African frogs that change gender as needed; Venus flytraps and other plants that attract and trap prey like animals; bacteria that feed on the toxic fumes from deep sea "black smokers"; birds like the Alpine Swift that almost never touch ground, and birds like the ostrich that never *leave* the ground; and much, much more.

Scientists help us see that the earth, and the entire cosmos, reflects the love of making new things that is the mark of its Creator.

Science helps religions meet their own goals

Medicine and the social sciences help religions understand people and how people are affected by religion itself. Sociology, anthropology, organization studies, psychology, and human biology have acquired a vast amount of information about what makes people tick. If a religious group wants its followers to be spiritually healthy, disciplined, open-minded, and compassionate, it makes sense to pay attention to research that shows what kind of relationships and experiences actually foster those qualities in people.

These disciplines also offer some excellent *tools* that religious groups can use. The Appreciative Inquiry and Asset-mapping processes I've done with fading congregations help them discover new vitality in their mission. These tools focus on what God is doing in their midst *now* (not just thirty years ago) and on the resources for ministry they *have* (not just those they've *lost*). It helps release faith groups from the mental straitjacket created by problem-focused anxiety.[11]

Oddly, few of the religious communities I am aware of regularly use social science tools to assess whether they are actually achieving their core purpose. They could host ethnographic-type interviews to find out which parts of their ministry have actually brought people closer to God, or fostered healing, or built loving relationships, or gave people hope, and so on. If a religion assumes that its mandate has been given to it by God, surely it would want to carry out that Divine mandate as *effectively* as possible. My suspicion, perhaps not fair but based on my own long involvement, is that sometimes religious leaders don't want to jeopardize the perks they get from their office by looking too closely at how well they are actually doing their job.

What Can People of Faith Learn from Science?

Many religious traditions have their roots in *revelation*, special knowledge given to a prophet by extraordinary means—an angel, a dream, a burning bush. Today, scientists are the new prophets. They tell us fantastic things about the nature of reality that are not evident to those who don't have their tools or training. Trusting them might seem much like a spiritual leap of faith, except that, unlike religious revelation, scientific discoveries can be *repeated* and *verified*. So it makes sense to take what the community of scientists say at least as seriously as the revelations of our religious leaders. Let's look at a few discoveries that have significant implications for religious belief and practice.

Deep time and space—finding our place in the universe

If you're a boomer, or a fan of 1960s cartoons, you might remember the TV show *The Flintstones*. This "modern stone-age family" apparently lived at the same time as the dinosaurs and managed to co-opt many of them into serving as earth-movers, pets, garbage disposals, and vacuum cleaners.

Strangely, this wonderfully anachronistic cartoon is not far off from the way in which some Christian groups have dealt with tensions between the biblical and scientific origin stories. Most well-known, perhaps, are the Creation Science folks whose museums (about twenty in the US, a couple in Canada, and one in Australia) have attracted media attention. In some way, all fans of creation science insist that dinosaurs and humans coexisted in the early years of an earth that was specially created by God six to ten thousand years ago.[12]

To be honest, that compressed view of time has been the default through human history. The ancients differed widely on their understanding of *how* the earth was created but not much on *when*. The *how* stories vary from the Cherokee account of a water beetle from the sky realm making the earth out of mud, to the Kubu people's tale of Mbombo vomiting up creation as a result of a stomach ache, to the Jewish and Christian insistence that Elohim spoke the universe into existence over six days.

But most cultures have imagined the *when* of creation within a fairly short time period—usually just far enough in the past to be beyond living memory but close enough to be relevant to current affairs.

The reason for this is unclear. In an experiment on time perception that I conducted at the University of Alberta in the seventies, I found that people tend to mentally perceive time the way computers allocate space for data: if there is a lot of data, a lot of space is allocated. Looking back over long stretches of time for which our brains have very little detailed data (so not much "storage space" is required), we automatically perceive the time period as small.

In the seventeenth and eighteenth centuries, this misperception of the age of creation was challenged by scientific observation. Careful observers wondered, "Why does the earth look so 'worn down' in places?" They could see that erosion and other natural processes are very slow and could not possibly, in just a few hundred or thousand years, have turned a young, crisp world into the one we see now.[13] And then the discovery of radiation at the end of the nineteenth century allowed for a reliable process of dating rocks based on the steady decay of radioactive isotopes. By various means, we came to understand that our earth is about 4.5 billion years old. And more recently, astronomers' observations of galactic movement have allowed us to date our expanding universe at about 13.7 billion years.

Scientists' discovery of the incomprehensible age of the earth and the universe ("deep time") has profound implications for the way religions think about human beings. To begin with, it reduces humanity's time in this universe to something like a period at the end of a thirty-volume encyclopedia. Writer John McPhee, who coined the term "deep time," notes we can really only think about deep time in metaphors like that. Compared to just the *earth's* age, he says, human history (even when assessed at about two million years) is like the instantaneous but brilliant explosion of a nuclear bomb, or like three minutes before midnight on the last (sixth) day of creation. McPhee says that if the earth's history were the length of a man's arms opened wide, all the time since the dinosaurs would be just the fingerprint on the tip of one extended middle finger, and "in a single stroke with a medium-grained nail file you could eradicate human history."[14]

Pretty humbling. Apparently, creation got along just fine without humans for about 99.9999 percent of its existence. It seems we're not essential to its functioning. And, given that most mammalian species last about two million years on average, humanity's "flash in the pan" lifespan may be almost up. Creation could go on for billions or even trillions more years without us.

Science also helps us see that humanity's footprint on the cosmos is small not only in time but also in space. Modern telescopes show us that just the *observable* universe is enormous. Present estimates are that it would take a beam of light, traveling at 186,000 miles per second, 93 *billion years* to cross it (and the *unobservable* universe is estimated to be at least 250 times larger!). Astrophysicist Ethan Siegel explains that if we had the time to count them, our best telescopes could see about 176 billion galaxies (each with thousands to billions of stars), but that is only about 10 percent of the 2 trillion that are calculated to actually be out there.[15]

On top of all that, astronomers are able to discern that many, perhaps most, of the stars in these galaxies have planets. NASA's count of the visible "exoplanets" in our neighborhood is over four thousand at the time of writing and growing rapidly. Many of them are Earth-like in size and distance from their star (in the "Goldilocks zone") and could conceivably support life, perhaps life as complex, or more complex, than our own.[16]

So here's the thing: If humans can interact with only an *infinitesimal* part of creation's spacetime, then what did God create all the rest of it *for*? Not just for us, obviously, if we can't see most of it, can travel to virtually none of it, and aren't around long enough to enjoy any significant amount of its beauty and danger!

Deep time and space also call into question humanity's impact on creation. Christian theology, for example, has often spoken of a "Fall"—a time at creation's beginning when humanity corrupted it. However, there is no scientific evidence of an idyllic period in the cosmos before *Homo sapiens* showed up. Great catastrophes (supernovas, for example, planetary collisions, or the vast meteor that struck the Yucatan Peninsula in Earth's more recent history) have been abundant throughout the life of the universe. And there is no evidence that such events increased in severity when we arrived on the scene.

In this, science helps religion stay humble. It reminds us that we are neither gods—the center and purpose of creation—nor demons—the architects of creation's destruction. Science counters the theological narcissism that assumes that God is really only interested in me and my group, and everyone else—the rest of the universe—is just wallpaper, created for us but ultimately destined for an eternal trash can. It also cautions us not to assume that our experience of God can be generalized to the rest of creation. We have no idea how God has dealt with anyone but ourselves—perhaps not even other species on this planet.

All that being said, discovering how vast our cosmos is can knock us into the other ditch—leave us feeling insignificant, worthless. Humans don't seem to flourish without a sense of value and purpose. Religion helps us keep our balance by insisting that God is *everywhere*, present at all scales of time and space, and cares about *everything*, from quarks to the multiverse—us humans included. Together, science and religion help us see that we are neither *in*significant, nor *all*-significant. As the Hebrew psalmist expresses it (Ps 8:3–5):

> When I look at the night sky and see the work of your fingers—
> the moon and the stars you set in place—
> what are mere mortals that you should think about them,
> human beings that you should care for them?
> Yet you made them only a little lower than God
> and crowned them with glory and honor.

The Big Bang—connections with religious origin stories

Modern astronomers are time travelers. Because the universe is so enormous, the light that reaches us from its outer regions has taken a very long time to get here. Imagine our ancient ancestors sending messages across the world on the back of slugs. We'd be getting them only now, millennia later. But through those messages we would see the world as it was thousands of years ago.

Similarly, as our ability to gather the faint light from distant regions of the universe increases, we can see how it has evolved over the eons. Turns out it has never been a stable, unchanging entity. For one thing, the universe is expanding rapidly. Projecting backward, scientists are confident that it began as an infinitely small, hot, dense superforce. In a tiny fraction of a second after its arrival, the fundamental forces—gravity, electromagnetism, and the forces that bind and repel particles inside an atom—formed and the universe inflated rapidly. Tiny ripples in this initial inflation eventually led to the unevenness in cosmic gases that allowed gravitational forces to condense them into stars and galaxies.

But the big bang was not accompanied by a "big flash"; the infant universe spent its first 380,000 years in the *dark*. It was too hot and dense even for light to escape. But as things cooled, stable atoms eventually formed, releasing energy as photons (light) in the process. This "primordial" light—the "Cosmic Microwave Background"—can still be detected by space telescopes (otherwise our atmosphere blocks it).[17]

At about two hundred million years, the first stars and galaxies began to coalesce. Initially they were composed of light elements, hydrogen and helium. But as stars aged, they exploded and reformed, developing and eventually scattering heavier elements that over time became the heart of rocky planets (like the earth).

Our own star formed from such recycled stellar remains about 4.6 billion years ago. Its entourage of starstruck celestial fans—the solar system—formed during the sun's first half billion years. The process was a kind of solar roller derby as young planets jockeyed for stable orbits through a violent series of gravitational bumps and collisions. The losers in that match were sidelined to the

Kuiper belt and the Oort cloud, a vast collection of comets, planetoids (like Pluto and Eris), and asteroids that extends far beyond the orbit of Neptune.

What significance then might the "Big Bang" have for faith and religion? When the Big Bang was first proposed by scientists, some Christians celebrated. If there was a bang, there had to be a bomb-maker—someone who set it off—they said. It's proof of a Creator! And then, in 1973, Australian physicist Brandon Carter proposed the "anthropic principle."[18] Carter noted that the basic "laws" of this universe are finely tuned to make life (such as ours) possible. He calculated that if the four fundamental forces in our universe were even slightly different, life would not be possible. For example, stars would never form, or if they did, would burn out too quickly for life to evolve. Considering all the different ways in which universes might be formed—or even start to form before they collapsed—our universe appears to be highly improbable.

To some people of faith, this was proof that our universe was "designed" by a supreme "Intelligence." But that is a misunderstanding. Carter wasn't religious. His theory is that there is a vast "multiverse" containing an infinite number of universes, only a few of which (perhaps only this one) have the conditions in which life can evolve. If that is the case, then obviously the fact that we are around to have this conversation means that we are in the universe that can sustain life.

Theologians of course can then reply, "Yes, but where did the multiverse, with its ability to host a life-bearing universe, come from?"

Neither idea—that our universe was created by God, or that we are part of an uncreated multiverse—is currently provable. However, neither idea is ridiculous. Certainly the Big Bang reinforces the assumption of many ancients that creation has a beginning.[19] However, it does not say anything about "who" or "if" anyone/thing caused it. Science is only concerned with how things work—the *internal* relationships within the universe.

Religions have a different focus. The core interest of religions is in the relationship creation has to its *external*[20] Source—its Creator. Religions want people to reimagine life's gifts, obligations, and dangers in light of their relationship to God.

For that reason, if there is any language in religious texts that appears to be "scientific," it is usually the science of ordinary sensory experience. In Genesis, for example, the sun is described just as we experience it—moving around the earth (not the earth around the sun as astronomers have discovered). The sky is spoken of as a high, rotating dome in which the stars are fixed and out of which the rain falls. The earth is a flat (not curved) surface beneath our feet. For the most part this is the only sensible way for authors of sacred texts to describe natural phenomena. If any ancient writer had precognitively read Einstein's mind and used the concepts of "spacetime relativity" in their creation stories, the texts would have been incomprehensible to the readers of every era (most of us moderns included!).

Having said that, occasionally sacred texts describe natural phenomena in unexpected ways that may jibe better with modern science than with our ordinary experience of them. For example, the Genesis 1 statement that "light" preceded the birth of the sun happens to agree with Big Bang science. That primordial light (the "Cosmic Microwave Background" I described earlier) appears about 380 thousand years after the Big Bang. But it's 200 million years *after that* before the first stars show up and about 9 billion years before our own sun is formed. Apparently, the light *did* come first.

Another example of religious-scientific convergence: Hindu yogis and prophets have long taught that the forests of the Himalayan mountain range are the matted hair of Lord Shiva, which softens and slows the annual torrential rains (said to be sent by the goddess Ganga to cleanse the earth). The result is the life-giving Ganges River. Now ordinary observation would suggest to those dwelling near the mountains that harvesting a little fire-wood—or even a lot—could not possibly harm the sacred river or even make a dent in the vast forest. Yet erosion of sediment into the Ganges has become a serious problem today as a result of centuries of overlogging. Modern science, in its warnings about forest management and erosion, echoes what Hindu teachers[21] had been saying, using the mythical image of Lord Shiva's hair, for a thousand years.

There are other implications of the Big Bang that I address in the chapter on "Why bad things happen"—for example, the fact that the early universe was formed in *darkness* or that the destructive force of supernovas was necessary for rocky planets that support life to form. These suggest that the Creator is God of the *darkness*, not just the light, and is God of *de*struction, not just *con*struction. In fact, as we'll see in that chapter, there seems to be a pattern of "cosmic recycling" in the universe where new and more complex elements require the breakdown and remaking of older, simpler forms. One might even say, using Christian terminology, that there is a "crucifixion-resurrection" pattern that constantly recurs throughout the history of the universe, our own earth, and even our own lives.

Decoding of the human genome

For the past two centuries biologists and paleontologists have been obsessed by the incredible discovery that, like the Big Bang, all life on this planet has a single point of beginning about 3.5 billion years ago. That conclusion followed from careful observation of the change in fossils through different ages of rock and sediment, from experiments with the mutation of short-lived species (like E. coli bacteria[22]) and, now most recently, with the ability to digitally map the genetic codes that govern life.

In 2003, the Human Genome Project identified the three billion base pairs of molecules (nucleotides) that make up the forty-seven thousand odd genes, grouped into twenty-three pairs of chromosomes, that compose the genetic instructions (the genome) that human cells use to grow and duplicate.[23] This discovery has made it possible to compare our genome to those of ancient hominin fossils. Carbon-dating of those fossils suggests that as a species, we *Homo sapiens* appeared in modern form about two hundred thousand years ago.

However, forerunners to *Homo sapiens* appear in the fossil records as far back as five to seven million years ago, when ape-like creatures in Africa began to walk on two legs. As with the evolution of other species, it seems that there was initially a good deal of experimentation. A number of hominin species emerged from the ancient great apes, some closely enough related that they could interbreed with each other.

Being able to trace our genetic code allows us to see that *Homo sapiens* have incorporated some DNA material from interbreeding with other ancient hominins (especially Neanderthals and Denisovans). It is also evident that all *Homo sapiens* are rather closely related to one another, tracing back to a small number—less than a thousand—breeding pairs in Africa (there is no consensus yet as to why the numbers dropped so low at that point).

Finally, the human genetic code turns out to be very similar to the genetic codes of other animals and even plants. Humans share 99.9 percent of their DNA with each other, but also share effectively 95 to 96 percent with chimpanzees and bonobos, and even 60 percent with *bananas*. In fact, no form of life on earth is completely unique. All life on earth appears to be deeply connected over a very long common history. So particular traits (such as size, color, types of sensory organs, even self-awareness, emotions, and the ability to reason and make ethical judgments[24]) exist on a continuum between species (including us) rather than as discrete abilities uniquely owned by a particular species.

What are some implications for faith of the discovery that all life on earth is connected in an evolutionary process? There are many of course. One of them, as already mentioned, is that there is no evidence for any "orders of creation"—that is, no permanent, separated cubby holes in which each species was created, properly belongs, and must always stay. Science's careful observations show us that life is fluid. So it is constant *change*—not a predetermined static natural order—that is the real norm. It suggests that religions should be careful about pronouncing that particular expressions of human life are "natural" or "God-ordained" and others are not.

A second implication has to do with humanity's relationship to *nonhuman* life. The Hebrew book of Genesis, for example, says that humans were created "in the image of God." This has conventionally been taken to mean that humans are holy in a unique and special way and that all other life forms are "profane"—that is, able to be used by humans without desecrating the divine image.

However, Genesis does not say "*only* humans were made in the image of God." We love to imply it, being quite impressed with ourselves and all. But the word "only" is not there. And while Genesis is obviously addressed to humans, it doesn't, in chapters 1 and 2 at least, say much about how everything else relates to God (though there is some of that later in chapter 11—when God makes a covenant with the land and its creatures).

Later biblical authors suggest that not just humans but *all* of creation in some way shares God's image. For example, John 1:3 ("All things came into being through him") was interpreted by ancient Christian theologians such as Irenaeus, St. Justin, and Francis of Assisi to mean that the Divine "Word" is the pattern for *all* of creation. Thinking of God as "trinity" (three Persons in one God), ancient Christians believed that the Father provides the source material for creation; it is funneled *through* the Son, who provides the pattern that ultimately gives all things their character and shape; and the Spirit energizes all things.

Here's the key: If all things are patterned on their Creator, then *everything, without exception, no matter how attractive, repulsive, useful, dangerous, or uninteresting it may be to humans,* reflects the life and character of God in some way.

The implication, as many indigenous religious traditions have insisted, is that we ought to treat all of the earth with respect and regard other entities as "sisters and brothers." In this, religion can help keep science ethical. If, as scientists themselves are realizing, other species share the capacity for self-sacrifice and altruism, for sustaining long-term friendships, and experiencing emotions such as grief, hope, pain, and sadness, then they ought not to be used for experimentation in a way that causes undue suffering.

A third implication of the discovery that life on earth is continuous is that it presses North American Christians who have been antagonistic to the idea of evolution to take a closer look at their own origin stories. Genesis chapters 1 and 2, for example, insist that humans come both from God (ultimately) *and* (more immediately) from the sea and the soil. They claim that God formed humans from *humus*, Adam from the *adamah* (Hebrew for "dirt"—Gen 2:7).

Sixteenth-century reformer Martin Luther said that the acts of God are "clothed in creation." Personally, I am delighted to imagine God working patiently through the earth's long processes of experimentation, mutation, and adaptation to bring forth wonderful new expressions of life. So, there is nothing inherently atheistic in assuming that creation itself has some freedom to experiment, to be creative like its Creator!

In addition, the discovery that we have Neanderthal and

Denisovan genes in our bodies may help Jews and Christians pay more attention to the fact that the Genesis texts speak of not only a *common* human origin (Genesis 1–3, Adam and Eve, Cain and Abel in the garden) but also of *diversity* in our origins (Gen 4:16–17, where Cain leaves the garden and finds a wife, and people sufficient to build a city, in the land of Nod).

So, we can see that both science and some ancient religious texts together challenge practices and philosophies that separate human beings and other creatures into categories that devalue some and allow them to be abused. And both science and religion—in their best expressions—offer a strong challenge to all forms of classism, racism, genderism, and so on.

Einstein's discovery of special and general relativity

In 1905 Einstein determined that space and time are interwoven into a single fabric. So, if I speed up my movement through space, I slow down my movement through time. This means that astronauts on the International Space Station age a little more slowly than we landlubbers because of the station's high orbital speed.

Einstein also discovered that time passes more slowly close to massive objects. So, the satellites that govern our GPS systems have to be carefully calibrated to take in the fact that they are moving faster than we are (so time slows for them) but are farther from the earth (so time is speeded up for them). It's a headache!

What is really significant for us, though, is that Einstein's theory (now well supported by experimental evidence) insists that all objects and forces in the universe act on each other to some degree. That means there is no universal background "stage" on which individual things play out their lives; space itself is in flux. Reality is a web of *relationships*, not a collection of individuals. In other words, *creation is simply one vast interconnected community of matter and energies*, affecting and being affected by each other.

This should not seem startling to religious people who believe that God is present everywhere in creation, that all things are connected in God, or even, as in Christian tradition, that *God is community* (Trinity). Nonetheless, many religious groups have put up walls of suspicion, even condemnation, between themselves and others.

But what if those of us who are religious took the interconnectedness of creation seriously? It might change how we practice our faith. For example:

- Religious ethics might begin with the well-being of *communities* (e.g., how particular kinds of relationships support or injure community well-being) rather than the personal purity or piety of individuals (which often just ends up in a game of religious one-upmanship). "Good" and "evil" would be seen as characteristics of *relationships*, not something individuals can own or be or do.

- Salvation—or "healing/wholeness" as the original terms are better translated—might no longer be treated as an afterlife reward for individuals, but as something that happens in interconnected systems (families, workplaces, towns, nations, and biosystems). Healing never happens independent of the relationships in which one is embedded.

- Religions could focus on the *connections* between their organization and the wider community, rather than trying to draw in sharper relief the fences that separate believers and unbelievers or church and world.

- Religious founders (Jesus, for example) could be presented not primarily in terms of how they are *unique* and unlike all others, but rather how they reveal God deep in the life of the world *everywhere.*

Einstein has given both science and faith a great gift in demonstrating that the universe is not just "one damned thing after another," not just an empty stage littered with discarded, disconnected elements, but is a dense fabric of relationships that are *thick* with meaning. And both science and faith are a search for meaning. Both seek to understand the nature of these relationships, to uncover hidden histories, delve into deep causes. Because of Einstein, neither science nor religion need worry about running out of work. Science, however, will always be somewhat more interested in exploring relationships that can be *measured,* and religion will always be more interested in exploring the relationship we have with the *Creator* of it all.

My hope is that they can spend more time in conversation with each other.

Explore!

1. What in this chapter was disturbing or surprising or difficult for you? Why?

2. Talk to someone who is active in a faith community and also works in science. If you don't know such a person, contact the leader of a local faith community and ask if they could refer you to such a person, and explain why. Then talk with that person and ask them if they will share with you a little about how their faith and science interact with each other.

3. Watch a movie about human-like robots (e.g., *Ex*

Machina or *The Machine* or *The Matrix*) with a friend. How do you react to the possibility that humans may be able to manufacture things that are a lot like us? How might our discussion of the connected and continuous nature of the universe be helpful (or not)? Discuss with your viewing partner how faith and science might help each other in the development of artificial intelligence.

Notes

1. David Masci, senior researcher, "Religion and Science in the United States," Pew Research Center, 2009, https://tinyurl.com/yhmcag7y.

2. *Stanford Encyclopedia of Philosophy*, s.v. "Religion and Science," https://tinyurl.com/yj2jhrna.

3. Francis Collins, *The Language of God: A Scientist Presents Evidence for Belief* (New York: Free Press, 2017).

4. Katharine Hayhoe, *A climate for change: Global warming facts for faith-based decisions* (New York: FaithWords, 2009).

5. Nidhal Guessoum, *The Young Muslim's Guide to Modern Science* (Manchester, UK: Beacon Books, 2017).

6. John Haught, *The New Cosmic Story: Inside Our Awakening Universe* (New Haven: Yale University Press, 2017).

7. Mani Bhaumik, *Code Name God: The Spiritual Odyssey of a Man of Science* (New Delhi: Penguin/Random House India, 2018).

8. Alan Wallace, *Contemplative Science: Where Buddhism and Neuroscience Converge* (New York: Columbia University Press, 2007).

9. John Polkinghorne, *Quarks, Chaos & Christianity: Questions to Science and Religion*, 2nd ed. (New York: Crossroad, 2005).

10. Jürgen Moltmann, *God in Creation: A New Theology of Creation and the Spirit of God* (Minneapolis: Fortress Press, 1993), 197.

11. Harder, *Discovering the Other*, 2013.

12. See one list of Creation Science museums at https://tinyurl.com/

ye8lhu9z.

13. Some creation science advocates I have known would respond by saying that the earth was created "looking old." They would argue that God created the earth a few thousand years ago and that the things we assume are signs of age simply reflect God's creative license.

14. John McPhee, *Annals of the Former World* (London: Farrar Straus Giroux, 1998), 89–91.

15. Ethan Siegel, "This Is How We Know There Are Two Trillion Galaxies in the Universe," *Forbes*, October 18, 2018, https://tinyurl.com/yeydqqpc. The two trillion number is the latest estimate by an international team of astronomers led by Christopher Conselice of the University of Nottingham.

16. *NASA Exoplanet Archive*, https://tinyurl.com/yctdw74x.

17. Identified in 1964 by American radio astronomers Robert Wilson and Arno Penzias, who called it "Cosmic Microwave Background" (CMB) radiation.

18. Brandon Carter, "Large number coincidences and the anthropic principle in cosmology," in M. S. Longair, ed., *Confrontation of Cosmological Theories with Observational Data* (Dordrecht Reidel Publishing Company, 1974), 291–98.

19. Hinduism is an exception in this regard. In general, its various traditions regard the world as being created and destroyed over and over, in an endless cycle.

20. Obviously God is not external in the sense that God is "outside" of the universe, since God inhabits every atom of it in the most intimate possible way. I mean "external" in the sense that God is not a creature, not part of the creation that science studies.

21. E.g., Shankaracharya (788–820 CE), scientist-yogi J. C. Bose (1858–1937). I once heard contemporary Indian ecologist Vandana Shiva use this myth in a lecture on protecting the Himalayan forests.

22. Richard Lenski and T. C. Burnham, "Experimental evolution of bacteria across 60,000 generations, and what it might mean for economics and human decision-making," *Journal of Bioeconomics* 20, no. 1 (April 2018), 107–24. Lenski has observed remarkable evolution of the bacteria in just twenty-eight years.

23. The number of genes the original project identified was just under 20,000, but deeper research has more than doubled that number since 2003 as the role of mitochondrial, RNA, and micro-RNA genes has been explored.

24. See Mark Bekoff and Jessica Pierce, *Wild Justice: The Moral Life of Animals*, University of Chicago, 2010; or Barbara King, "The Orca's Sorrow," *Scientific American*, 320, no. 3 (March 2019), 30–35.

7

Where Is God When Bad Things Happen?

In Stephen King's screenplay for the TV series *Storm of the Century*, Mike the narrator says:

> You know the story about Job? In the Bible? Well here's the part that never got written down . . . Job gets down on his knees and says, "Why did you do this to me, God? All my life I worshipped you, but you destroyed my livestock, blighted my crops, killed my wife and my children, and gave me a hundred horrible diseases . . . all because You had a bet going with the Devil? Well, okay . . . but all your humble servant wants to know is—*Why me?*" So he waits, and just when he's about made up his mind God isn't going to answer, a thunderhead forms in the sky, and lightning flashes, and this voice calls down: "*Job! I guess there's just something about you that pisses me off.*"[1]

Have you ever felt like God, or the Universe, had it in for you? Like Someone up there was pissed off at you for no particular reason?

I felt that way a few years ago. Over a fifteen-month period the following happened to our family: our youngest son was mugged, stabbed, and almost murdered in three separate incidents; I contracted a deadly amoebic infection in Tanzania that almost killed me; my brother ran into a train at night in the fog and survived that, but shortly afterwards his car was totaled again by a tow truck; my dad got bowel cancer and had to have an operation; my mom was also diagnosed with cancer. No one actually died, but the fallout from each of those incidents has permanently changed our family.

During the long northern winter nights, I lay awake feeling as though an evil entity had wrapped its talons around our family's neck—and God hadn't noticed, or perhaps even approved. That dark night of my soul led me to think carefully about what I expected from God.

God as Santa Claus and Bodyguard

I realized that deep down I'd assumed that the main point of connecting with God is to gain some benefit, some "good," for ourselves or those we care about. It's common in Western society to portray God this way—as a Divine Vending Machine, the ultimate dispenser of all good things. (I suppose in our capitalist culture religion would be a hard sell if it didn't!)

The good we desire might be positive. Our Saskatchewan Roughriders quarterback recently said he was able to play with an injured ankle because he had prayed and been "sprinkled by Jesus." Athletes pray for a win, students pray for success on a school exam or help in finding a summer job, farmers pray for rain for their crops, mourners pray that the dying will be ushered into eternal life.

The "good" we desire might also be some form of protection—from accidents during travel, from online bullying, from danger, disease, the devil, and hell.

Is this the essence of faith—trying to get what we want from a Divine Giver? If so, then those with a long history of active religious practice may justifiably feel betrayed by God when suffering hits them. They may feel, as I did, that they had an unspoken agreement with God: "If I worship you, behave myself, and do good, then you'll look after me." So when the bad times hit, what happened? Did God break the agreement, or did I? Is God punishing me for not measuring up? That's what I heard from many of the farmers who went bankrupt in the 1980s and 1990s (as I was doing my doctoral research[2]): "I'm so ashamed. God must be angry with me. What have I done wrong?"

Even those who haven't had an active religious life may expect that the universe will protect them, or provide what they want, if they just find the right key. Baseball players are infamous for believing that certain behaviors will help them win: for example, wearing a necklace made of hunted animal teeth (Turk Wendell), sleeping with one's bat (Richie Ashburn), carrying a pouch of minerals in one's pocket (Steve Finley), or covering one's batting helmet with pine tar (Vladimir Guerrero).

Apart from superstition, many expect that they will be secure as long as they have high social status, a good job, a good name, an intact family, or the perfect diet. It's a shock when these things fail and life tumbles into the toilet.

The Prosperity Gospel

Let's check out the assumptions of the religious folks first. Has God really agreed to be our personal Santa Claus/bodyguard? Prosperity gospel evangelists think so (some are connected to the "miracle-workers" I mentioned in an earlier chapter). Wikipedia has a useful description:

> Prosperity theology (sometimes referred to as the *prosperity gospel*, the health and wealth *gospel*, the *gospel* of success, or seed faith) is a controversial religious belief among some Protestant Christians, who hold that financial blessing and physical well-being are always the will of God for them, and that faith, positive speech [that is,

speaking as though there is no doubt that they will receive what they ask for], and donations to religious causes will increase one's material wealth. Prosperity theology views the Bible as a contract between God and humans: if humans have faith in God, he will deliver security and prosperity.[3]

Prosperity gospel proponents such as Oral Roberts and Kenneth Copeland—or more recently, Joel Osteen, Benny Hinn, Creflo Dollar, and Joyce Meyers—owe their success in part to the adage that "nothing succeeds like success." They tell their followers, "If you give *us* money, God will make *you* rich." Then they point to their own wealth as evidence that it works. It doesn't, of course. It's a pyramid scheme with a religious overlay. But like all pyramid schemes (and many lotteries), people want to believe they can get rich quick. Unfortunately, the only ones who actually get rich are the evangelists and their staffs who got in on the ground floor.[4]

In 2007, US Senator Charles Grassley launched an investigation into televangelists, looking at whether they violated IRS rules about excessive compensation for leaders of religious non-profits. However, strong pushback from evangelical Christian lobby groups silenced most witnesses, and there were no definitive findings of wrongdoing.[5]

Of course, most people of faith don't buy into that extreme view of God as one's financial patron. But as Evangelical teacher Beth Moore notes, even those who reject the prosperity gospel may still embrace a "pampering gospel"—one that makes them feel safe and keeps them in their comfort zones.[6]

Why do we do that? What's behind our insistence on seeing God as a fairy Godmother who will grant our deepest wishes? I wonder if it is the assumption that suffering is inherently *evil*—that a holy and loving God would get rid of it.

Is It Reasonable to Imagine a World without Suffering?

A believer might assume that God can do *anything* because God is all-powerful. But God's power serves God's will. And there are some things sheer power simply can't do. For example, many religious traditions assert that God wants people to freely love God. If that is actually God's will, then God *must not* (unlike Star Trek's Captain Picard) "make it so." If God did that, people's affection would be coerced; it wouldn't be real love. People must be given the freedom to fall in love or to refuse God's courtship.

So then the question of whether suffering can be erased depends on what kind of universe God wants. Presumably the universe God wants (at least for now) is the universe God actually made. We've seen something of its nature in the previous chapter: it is dynamic, creative, experimental, deeply connected, constantly evolving. So is it possible to avoid all suffering in such a cosmos?

I'd have to say no. Whether you believe in God or not, there are tensions in the universe we actually have that make suffering *inevitable*. Here are just a few.

One person's trash is another's treasure

I saw a cartoon by Man Martin where a choir member is singing the hymn, "All things bright and beautiful, all creatures great and small, all things wise and wonderful, the Lord God made them all." A rat interrupts him and says, "You left out a verse." His friends—a snake, skunk, and spider—fill in, singing:

> Things that blight and putrify, all parasites and lice,
> all things weird and horrible, not just the stuff that's nice;
> every mildew spore that blossoms, flesh-eating virus too,
> maggots on the roadkill were made by You-know-who!
> All things gross and poisonous, all buzzards in the sky,
> God made ticks with Lyme disease, although we can't say why.

Shocked, the choir member says, "That will *never* make it into the hymnal." The rat replies "Maybe not *your* hymnal."[7]

You see the point. What is agreeable to one may be quite disagreeable to another. A garbage dump is noxious to nearby suburbanites but a smorgasbord to flies and seagulls. A long spell of hot dry weather may be delightful to tourists and urban sunbathers but frightening to farmers whose livelihood depends on rain. A single swipe of antiseptic may protect a homemaker, but it kills millions of microbes. The hiring of a new employee can be exhilarating for the one hired but crushing for the candidate who was rejected. A star that goes supernova destroys the planets in its system and damages others up to thirty light years away, but its shock waves may also jolt gas clouds into forming new stars, and it throws off the heavy elements necessary for life. In this diverse universe, *one creature's suffering is another's celebration*. It's hard to imagine how it would be possible for all creatures to have everything they like unless each existed in its own separate reality.

God recycles: for new things to develop, old things must break down

According to the prophet Isaiah (45:7) God says, "I form light and create darkness, I make weal and create woe." Hebrew literature speaks not only of the "Angel of the Lord" in a positive sense but also of the "*Destroying* Angel" (for example Exod 12:23; 2 Sam 24:15; Job 33:22). In Hinduism, the supreme God-force Brahman expresses itself in three gods in tension: as Brahma the Creator, as Shiva the Destroyer, and as Vishnu the Preserver.

In the end, most religious traditions acknowledge that the Creator must take final responsibility for *all* of creation. It's obvious that light and dark, breaking down and building up, harm to one and blessing to another, is occurring constantly. A God who is all-powerful, and everywhere, is ultimately responsible for *both*.

So even if "hordes of devils fill the land, all threatening to undo us," as Christian reformer Martin Luther claims in his hymn "A Mighty Fortress Is Our God," any such forces of "undoing" must still answer to God.

Here's the problem God has: It's one thing to create something from nothing. But what do you do with creation once you've got it? It's like getting a Lego set for Christmas. My kids would quickly assemble the model on the box front. But what then? They couldn't start another project until they disassembled the old one. Now God could have built our universe in a final, fixed, frozen state and left it like a beautiful model on a shelf in the multiverse. But you know how great artists are—they get restless, always coming up with new ideas. If God is not only creative but, as we have seen, has also built a creative urge into the universe itself, then rearranging and recycling is *essential*. New stuff requires the disassembly of the old.

I saw this when I traveled in India. Scattered across the landscape were "half-houses." People would take the bricks from old homes to build new ones. I never knew if the houses I saw were coming or going.

A similar deconstruction-reconstruction dynamic is everywhere around us, at every scale in the universe. The sun that greets us each morning as the earth rotates is an engine of destruction—a ten-billion-year fire, slowly consuming a vast collection of cosmic gases. As it converts hydrogen to helium to iron, Sol releases energy, which strikes our planet. That energy is absorbed by plants and converted into organic material. Not being green (like Kermit), we humans can't soak up solar energy directly. So we throw the plants into our body's internal fire. Microbes in our gut break them down, and they burn in the mitochondrial furnaces captured by our cells in the distant past. As the plants disintegrate, they release into our bodies the energy they had captured from the sun, allowing us to build muscle, bone, and brain. Sooner or later, we die too, and microbes, plants, and animals break us down to release that solar energy, so *they* can live. To some extent it's *The Lion King*'s "circle of life."

Deconstruction is not only necessary to recycle energy; it also *makes room*. This winter a new granddaughter was born to us, and I realized that we didn't have a space in our house that would accommodate a baby's parents and baby paraphernalia. I had to tear down my office and rebuild in order to give the young family an adequate place.

Similarly, old institutions, cultural attitudes, and religious traditions at times need to crumble, so there will be room in people's hearts and lives for something new (we hope better). "No one puts new wine in old wineskins; otherwise the wine will burst the skins," Jesus once said when he was criticized for not strictly following the sabbath laws (Mark 2:22).

We humans owe our existence to the earth's capacity to make room. The demise of the dinosaurs made room for little mammals to crawl out of their holes and evolve into humans. And generation after generation of humans has gone to the grave, making room for fresh-eyed children. And thank God it is so! If we all lived forever, the earth would be quickly overrun by very senior citizens. Other species would be edged out of existence, and eventually there would be no place even for our own children. Having been swept off my feet by our new granddaughter, I know for sure that's not a world I'd *want* to live in.

This is not to say that all destruction leads obviously or automatically to new construction. We are all appalled by truly horrific annihilation—from earthquakes to the Holocaust. But death, entropy, chaos, evil—whatever you want to call the forces of destruction—they never have the last word. In part, this is because the more aggressive the destruction, the more quickly it runs out of fuel; ultimately, chaos eats itself. But more importantly to the eyes of faith, there appears to be at the base of this universe, surrounding and within it, a great Becoming, a Womb of enormous potential, that coaxes new forms of being out of the ashes of the old.

What makes life worth living also makes us suffer

The best things in life *aren't* free. They come with a price. For example:

- *Belonging:* In the biblical story of human origins (Genesis 1–4) the earthling—"Adam"—is lonely.[8] Loneliness is extremely painful. It's one of the most potent forms of suffering (which is why prisoners hate solitary confinement so much). God eases loneliness by giving Adam a partner and giving the couple children. Community forms, they belong. But that process guaranteed that they would suffer even more, because the love that draws the family together also makes them ache when they have to be apart or when one rejects the other, as Cain and Abel did. Passionate love suffers. Jesus suffered (Latin *passio*) because the people he passionately loved, with whom he wanted to belong, rejected him (John 1:11).

- *Diversity:* Adam and Eve's children are different. Abel is a rancher; Cain is a farmer. Difference is part of what attracts people to each other. A variety of gifts and perspectives can make an effective team or a resilient community. The apostle Paul recognizes this in 1 Corinthians 12 when he says that the body is not one member but many different members. Its unity comes from *integrated diversity*, not from uniformity ("If the whole body were an eye, where would the hearing be?" he jokes in verse 17). Abdu'-Baha, former head of the

Bahá'í faith, compares diversity to music where "different notes blend together in the making of a perfect chord."[9]

But difference also generates discord and conflict. It's not easy to manage. Between Cain and Abel, the differences led to envy and ultimately murder (Genesis 4). It is hard to understand and live with those who differ from us. Every married couple knows this, as does every community that welcomes immigrants and refugees. Some conflict is unavoidable.

- *Becoming.* As a professor I was responsible for helping students become pastors. That "becoming" is a good thing. But in order to *become* something more, my students had to *struggle*—to read a lot (some of it boring); travel to Saskatoon, leaving families for weeks at a time; write scary tests; take social risks preaching to groups and counseling troubled folk; and so on.

  Similar costs are evident all through our lives as we develop. Children skin their knees learning how to walk and ride a bike. Athletes put up with muscle soreness to build stronger bodies. New parents suffer severe sleep deprivation for months. This sort of struggle has been the constant companion of life on earth through its long evolutionary development. Granted, that struggle has ultimately led to remarkable things—whales, opera, rainforests, the Beatles. But the total suffering involved in getting here has been truly unimaginable.

Belonging, diversity, and becoming are also in tension with *each other.*[10] For example, in many families around the world parents have expectations about the life their children will lead. They may be expected to take over the farm or become a doctor, be heterosexual or gender-blind, live close to family or get out on their own as soon as possible. Those expectations put children in a bind. Their need to *belong* may be so powerful that it overwhelms their need to *become* or to be *diverse*. So they conform to their "tribe's" expectations but live frustrated, unhappy lives. Or their need to *become* may lead them to leave and chase their dreams, but in the end they don't find a place where they really *belong*. Either way, some suffering is inevitable.

So suffering is *not* avoidable. But for people of faith, that still leaves us with the question of God's involvement. We still have to ask: Does God sometimes send suffering as punishment (or relieve it as reward)? Does God even notice our suffering, or care?

What Is God's Role in Suffering?

The Creator, of course, doesn't have to answer to us. As God says in response to Job's complaints about his misfortunes, "Were you there when I made all this? Do you order the lightning, feed the lions, call up the dawn, send a flood, walk on the ocean floors?" (Job 38–42, from which I've compressed the ideas).

But that doesn't stop us from asking. A friend of mine, a young teen, wondered with anguish where God was when her uncle died. He was making arrangements for a group of seminarians to visit an aid agency overseas when his taxi was caught in a traffic accident and he was killed. I was asked to preach at the uncle's memorial service (I'll call him "Lorne"). Here is an extended segment from that sermon, responding to our question:

> Maybe you felt horrified, as I did, that God would allow a good man to be cut down so ignobly while he was on a mission of hospitality. Lorne wasn't perfect of course—life had dealt him some sickness, struggles and scars. But he was a man who gave his life unselfishly to care for others. So maybe you feel a little angry at God: "God, where were you when Lorne needed you?" Or even a bit of fear: "If

God doesn't protect and care for a man like Lorne, why would God protect and care for me?"

I can't tell you what God was thinking when Lorne was killed. But I do know a couple of things. One thing I know is that Lorne isn't the first good person to suffer like this. We've been listening to a story much like his all through Lent and Easter: the story of Jesus. It's about a good man, a man whose life was centered on love for others, a good man cruelly cut down in his prime. And his friends and family were just as shocked and mystified as we are tonight. Even Jesus himself cried out as he died, "My God, my God, why have you forsaken me?!"

Christians often try to rationalize Jesus' death by saying "well, he suffered *instead of us*." And maybe in some ways that's so. But more importantly for me, he suffered *like* us. The same kind of freakish bad things that happen to us, happened to Jesus.

You know the story: First Jesus' mother gets pregnant with him out of wedlock. Then just when she's about to give birth the governor decides to force everyone to travel back to their hometowns for a tax registry. So . . . nine months pregnant, walking to Bethlehem, and when they get there, their family won't take them in and the motel is full, so Jesus is born in some random animal pen. Then Mary and Joseph finally get a room in a house, and the foreign magi who want to visit go to the wrong guy for directions—to King Herod—who thinks a competitor for his throne has been born and sends out soldiers to kill all the Bethlehem babies. Jesus and family barely escape, and end up refugees in Egypt. A few years later Herod dies and Jesus' family comes back to Israel only to find a civil war raging between Herod's brothers as they vie for the throne. Then Jesus' dad—Joseph—dies young and leaves Jesus to care for his mother and siblings. After Jesus finally starts his ministry, he barely escapes being thrown off a cliff by jealous neighbors. His cousin John is beheaded. His good friend Lazarus dies unexpectedly. And in the end, Jesus is executed by local officials who were afraid that his popularity would stir up a revolution and bring down the wrath of Rome on their heads.

Unfair? Absolutely. Freakish? For sure. In just 33 years Jesus became a veteran of bad accidents. So you can understand why Jesus—who had been told at his baptism that he was God's beloved Son—why he cried out as he died "My God, my God, why have you forsaken me?!"

I don't know about you, but I've felt like that several times—forsaken by God. I know many people of faith do. Just because we're religious does not mean we're immune to bad stuff. Truth is, bad stuff happens to *everybody*—sometimes in great clumps that make us feel as if the sky has opened up and is raining cow pies on us.

So when your life gets messed up—know that you're in very good company—with Jesus, with Job and the prophets, with Mary, Paul and the early Christians, with God's people through the centuries, with every one of us here today. We can *all* relate. You're not alone in your suffering.

I think it's fair to say that it's not just a few good folks like Job or Jesus that have suffered a great deal. It's been the experience of key leaders in every religious tradition. Muhammad's father died before he was born, his mother died when he was six, and three of Muhammad's sons died in childbirth. The Buddha's ascetic advisors abandoned him. Moses struggled with betrayal, hunger, and war. Paul was shipwrecked, mugged, hungry, and cold. Israel's prophets were killed by King Saul. All of the Christian apostles ended up in jail. And of course in most religious traditions, there is a long list of martyrs—people who died at the hands of others when they confessed their faith. It's an illustrious bunch of sufferers!

So: If suffering is a sign of Divine disfavor, that means all of our great religious founders were God-cursed and we would be foolish to treat those folks as reliable spiritual guides.

But there is no indication that their suffering was divine punishment. They suffered for the same reasons we all do—because of random illness and accidents, because of decisions they made that have unfortunate if unforeseen consequences, and because other people hurt them. And these founders often disturbed folks at the top of their social pyramid who were privileged by the current arrangements and did not want to see the status quo upset. For example, Jesus's words and actions were perceived to be an instigation to revolt that threatened to bring down the wrath of the Roman army on Israel. It so worried local religious and political leaders that they plotted, and eventually carried out, his arrest (see Matt 12:14; John 11:47–48; Mark 3:6; 11:18; 12:12).

Clearly then, religious people are not specially protected by God. Neither do scoundrels seem to be specially singled out by God for punishment. History provides a long list of reprobates who were narcissistic, brutal, greedy, manipulative, or addicted to power in some form or other but didn't get what we thought they deserved.[11] While many who "live by the sword die by the sword," lots also live long in luxury with few tragedies and many enviable privileges.

Honestly, there is no evidence of a Divinely organized tit-for-tat. Neither a judgmental God nor a neutral universe seems to be dishing out what is popularly (though inaccurately) called "karma." What goes around doesn't always come around. Good deeds aren't always rewarded; bad deeds aren't always punished by suffering.

Yet people still want to believe in some sort of cosmic balance. So sometimes they make ridiculous associations. I've heard folks say, "I woke up sick this morning; I know it's because I flipped that guy off in traffic yesterday" or "I ran over my dog; I know it's because I forgot to water the pastor's plants, and they all died." It should be easy to see that these things are not related. Just because something occurs in the same time period or in sequence with something else does not mean one *causes* the other. Associations like that (which unfortunately occur too often in scientific reporting) are not evidence for cause and effect. That sort of reasoning is how most superstitions develop.

Now there are others who can see that things don't balance out in *this life*, but they hope that the scales will balance in an *afterlife*. Well, more often perhaps they hope that their *enemies* (not they themselves) will suffer and that they personally will be rewarded. But again—there's no *evidence* for such a balancing act beyond death. Experimentally, the afterlife is out of our reach. We can't send drones in to check it out, and those who die can't report. In any case, it's hard to understand how eternal punishment (adding an eternity of torture onto someone's bad deeds) could possibly "balance" anything. That just ramps up the destruction. If there is such a thing as eternal balance, wouldn't it be better reached by adding grace and healing to all the harms that have been done?

What about "acts of God"? Does God punish communities?

To this point we have been talking mostly about the suffering of individuals. But a great deal of suffering is *communal*. Large-scale disasters are big news these days. Earthquakes on the west coast of North America and hurricanes on the east coast, monsoon floods in India, blazing wildfires in Australia and western Canada, a deadly tsunami in Indonesia, volcanic eruptions in Guatemala and Hawaii, heat waves in Pakistan, Europe, and even the Arctic. Events on this scale affect thousands of people, dozens of communities.

It is common in Canada and the United States to refer to such disasters as "Acts of God." There is a 2001 movie starring Billy Connolly called *The Man Who Sued God*. In it, a man's only real possession—his fishing boat—is destroyed by lightning. He discovers that insurance won't cover it, since it's an act of God—so the guy sues several religious groups, figuring if it was really God's fault, God's front men should pay. Interesting movie.

Insurers use the term "Acts of God" to describe all those unpredictable, unavoidable things that "nature" (another of God's front men, apparently) dishes out. When insurance companies refuse to pay out for such events or require extra premiums to cover them, they send a dark message to afflicted communities: "This bad thing that happened to you folks was sent by God. It's God's will, maybe even God's punishment. Clearly, God wanted you folks to suffer. Who are we to stand in God's way—to try to undo God's judgment by paying money to God's victims?"

Religious traditions have struggled with large-scale disasters. The power in such events is easily associated with God. And the *indiscriminate* destruction they cause has always seemed unjust to believers. So, there is a tension in the ancient texts. On the one hand writers assumed that God must have had a good reason for allowing or causing the disaster (that is, the people *sinned*). So, the flood in Genesis is attributed to God as a punishment for humanity's—unspecified—evil (Gen 6:5–22). Similarly, in Genesis, the destruction of Sodom and Gomorrah is attributed to God's punishment of those cities for their sin (Gen 18:20–19:24). And there are similar warnings of impending destruction to cities and countries (e.g., Zeph 3:6; Micah 5:11; Jer 48:8). The Qur'an also speaks of God using natural disasters to punish sinful communities (e.g., al-Hajj 22:42–45).

On the other hand, however, ancient writers were convinced that God is *merciful*. So, there is also a protest stream in the sacred texts that clashes with the punishment motif. Abraham protests the destruction of Sodom and Gomorrah, and God agrees not to destroy them if there are ten righteous (Gen 18:32). In Genesis 9, God covenants not to flood the earth again. The Hebrew prophet Isaiah has God promising the nation: "When you pass through the waters, I will be with you; And through the rivers, they shall not overwhelm you for . . . you are precious in my sight, and honored and I love you" (Isa 43:2–4). And the Qur'an insists that Allah is merciful and *does not* punish people as they deserve (Fatir 35:45).

Perhaps the most we can honestly say is this: Disasters have multiple causes. Some of them *may* relate to community decisions, such as settling in dangerous locations (flood plains, unstable mountainsides, etc.), failing to pay attention to warning signs (of an impending storm, earthquake, or eruption), or severely depleting/damaging natural resources.

It is also good to remember that we are tiny creatures on a planet in a solar system that has its own rhythm of life and is not accountable to, or particularly aware of, us. Often, like fleas on a dog, we just end up along for the bumpy ride.

As far as *God's* involvement is concerned, however, there is simply no good *historical* evidence that God dishes out suffering to communities, anymore than to individuals, to punish them for bad behavior.

So, is suffering simply random?

No. Obviously ordinary cause and effect are at work. Creation has both freedom and predictability woven into it at all levels. And that's good. We need some predictability in order to survive—to count on the sun coming up in the morning, gravity holding us firmly on the earth, seeds sprouting in the springtime. So, it is the case, not always, but often, that we *do* reap what we sow. Often when we study hard, we get better grades; if we smoke, we're more likely to get lung cancer; those we treat with kindness often reciprocate; and when we gamble a lot, we tend to lose our shirts.

But the universe is also full of surprises—both horrifying and delightful. Because the universe is so intricately connected, even across quantum and galactic scales of size, every effect has many causes, going back eons, and every cause has effects far into the future. So, the future is more like a field of possibilities than a predictable straight line. And that's great—*new* things can happen, life can *evolve*. But that also means we can't plan a perfectly safe, happy life, free of suffering, no matter what kind of relationship we have with God.

If suffering then is built into the nature of a dynamic, evolving universe, what is God's role? This leads to our key question.

Where Is God When We, When the World, Suffers?

Perhaps another excerpt from that sermon for Lorne's memorial might get us started:

> There is a second thing I know. Jesus may have felt forsaken on the cross, but his very last words before he died were these: "Father, into your hands I commend my Spirit."
>
> You see, Jesus had discovered a secret. Over his 33 years Jesus found that no matter what curves life threw at him, the Father's hands were always there to catch him. That's what Jesus discovered when he and his fishing crew almost drowned in a sea storm. That's what Jesus discovered at Lazarus's tomb, and in the Garden of Gethsemane.
>
> This is the secret: that *God does not design the bad stuff in our lives; but God can help us redeem it.* There is no evidence that our Creator is a puppet-master, writing the script for every line in our lives, pulling our strings, spooling out a fate we can't escape. Instead God seems to allow real freedom in the world for the kind of freakish stuff that took Lorne's life.
>
> There's freedom for things to break. But when they do, when Jesus's life broke, he always found the Father's hands beneath him to catch the pieces, holding him, remolding him. That was true even, especially, after Jesus's death. As Jesus lay in that cold lonely tomb, God forged from his shattered body the risen Christ, the first of what Paul says will be a new humanity.
>
> That seems to be God's genius—making gorgeous quilts out of the scraps of our lives, making wonderful mosaics from the broken pieces of creation, working in everything—including the bad and the ugly—for good, as Paul says in Romans 8:28.
>
> I know we can't see the finished product of God's creation yet—anymore than Jesus or his friends could, in their own grief and agony.
>
> But I think we can say with confidence, based on the experience of our ancestors in the faith, that when that truck hit Lorne God was there. God's hands tenderly cradled his broken body, God wrapped Lorne's spirit in the arms of Divine Fatherly, Motherly love. And I

believe that's where Lorne rests, with sisters and brothers of every color and tribe.

God does the same for us now. "Peace I leave with you," Jesus says to his followers. The Aramaic word he uses is *shalom*—wholeness. Jesus promises us wholeness. Our broken hearts will be whole because, just like Lorne, who would move in to care for people who were hurting, God moved in with us, at Pentecost. God's Spirit surrounds us, holds us, is always there to help and to heal.

Father, into your hands, we commend our spirits.

Where is God when we suffer? Well, I assume that God is everywhere, in and through everything. If that's so, then imagine . . . God must feel it *all:* the pain of every blow struck in anger; the fiery immolation of a planet that falls into its sun; the death of a cell; the decay of a Higgs boson into quarks. God suffers every moment of this universe's deconstruction, every dying, dissolving, dismantling. God *suffers* the struggles of this universe, just as we suffer our own small part of it, because it is God's beloved child, and God wants it to grow into all that it can become.

I suspect that gives God an intimate empathy for our pain that no one else can possibly have. It means that when we cry out to God in anguish, we are not pounding on the closed door of a busy Deity (as C. S. Lewis, in his book *A Grief Observed*, says he felt after his wife's death).[12] Rather, our tears mingle with God's; God's heart pulses with ours. The pain is fully shared—perhaps not removed, but not borne alone.

It also means that in choosing this sort of relationship to creation, God has also chosen to be *weak, vulnerable*. The ancient Christian writers called it "kenosis"—self-emptying (as in Philippians 2). God chooses to be weak so that creation can grow strong.

You may have seen this dynamic in the workplace. A new employee is carefully trained and supervised, but gradually the supervisor steps back to give the employee room to try their stuff. That's the risky time. Same with our kids as they graduate from high school. We step back so they can step out. In the garden, we remove the protection from our seedlings, so they can "harden off" and adapt to the cold spring air. As a grandpa, I sometimes express uncertainty about trying a new thing (a slide, or zip-line), so my granddaughter will pluck up her courage and step forward to help me. My weakness gives her room to be strong. God's weakness, God's self-emptying, gives us room to grow into something more.

How Then Do We Deal with Suffering?

I said in the sermon that "God does not design our suffering, but God does help us redeem it." I don't mean that in a Pollyanna way. When we are wounded, scars remain (as they did for Jesus, even after his resurrection). Trauma from accident, illness, or abuse can leave us with debilitating triggers for the rest of our lives. So suffering, especially deep trauma, isn't "good for us" in some simplistic way.

On the one hand, suffering can squeeze our heart, turn us inward to protect ourselves from further injury, like a porcupine rolling up into a ball. In these "rolled up" times, nursing our wounded selves, we are least able to receive healing, most likely to despair. Shame paralyzes us; we don't feel presentable to the world, because we are not whole.

On the other hand, I have seen how individuals and communities in crisis have experienced some redemption of their suffering when they have found the courage to *open up*—to God's presence, to the neighbor's help or need, to the future as potentially good. That's when healing can happen—and sometimes unexpected transformation as well.

Openness can mean giving up the security we have invested in something or someone and *trusting God* to take care of us, no matter what or who we lose. It can mean releasing our pride to ask for help or to share our struggle with another sufferer. It can mean seeing through God's eyes—seeing other people, species, plants, places as *beloved*—and being *outraged* when they are intentionally damaged. And (hardest of all for some), it can mean seeing ourselves as God's beloved when others hurt us. So we *reject the shame* we feel and *muster our courage* to block the other from harming us further, while at the same time we *let go of our desire for revenge.*

Finally, redeeming suffering means leaving our options truly open, not treating the future as a dark tunnel shrinking into a black hole of oblivion, but trusting that we will find new purpose in life.

I saw how this dynamic of opening to God, neighbor, and future transformed the suffering of an elderly woman I visited in hospital. I'll call her Alice. She was curled up in bed, hooked up to various tubes. When I asked her how she was doing she sighed, "I just want to die." She told me that she had no family, no close friends; she was in a lot of pain and just had no reason to live. I told Alice I suspected God still had some purpose for her life and asked her if she had time to listen. I said, "Sometimes patients or staff will come into your room who have pain in their lives too. I'll bet a caring word from you and listening ear would help them." Then I asked if she had time to pray. I said, "I'm so busy, I don't always take much time to talk with God. But if you have time to pray, you can move God's hands and change the world." Shortly afterward I left (not my best pastoral visit to be honest!).

Three weeks later, I got a call from Alice. She was back in her care home and asked if I'd stop by. When I arrived, she opened the door, but I almost didn't recognize her. Alice was dressed up, smiling, had makeup on—she was *radiant.* I said, "Alice, you look great! What's happened?" She said, "Well, after your visit in the hospital, they wheeled a teenage girl into my room. I could hear her sniffling, and I remembered what you said about listening. So, I took my IV pole over to her bed and said, 'Honey, what's the matter?' She said, 'I just want to die.' I said, 'me too.' So we sat together and cried for a bit. You know, Sally—that's her name—and I got to be friends over the next couple of weeks in the hospital. And after we got out, Sally's been coming to visit me."

Then Alice went over to her coffee table and showed me a sheet covered with penciled names. "We have tea, and Sally tells me about her high school friends. I write down their names and pray for them. And I've been getting the newspaper. There are so many things to pray for!"

In sharing their desire to die, Alice and Sally experienced resurrection.

Well, that's my small bit on suffering. There are certainly no simple answers. If you want to pursue this question, I owe a great debt to theologian Douglas John Hall, who sums up various approaches to understanding suffering in his book *God and Human Suffering*.[13]

Perhaps for a person of faith, though, the best response to Job's question (at the beginning of this chapter) is from theologian C. S. Lewis: "I know now, Lord, why you utter no answer. You are yourself the answer. Before your face questions die away. What other answer would suffice?"[14]

Explore!

1. Talk to someone who works in a health care profession. Ask them how people cope with the pain and suffering they are going through. What have they noticed that seems to be helpful? What isn't helpful?

2. Discuss with a family member: What types of suffering (social, physical, mental) do you struggle with the most? Why are they so difficult to cope with? Are there any

mental/spiritual practices that help you deal with them?

3. How do you feel about the idea of a God who recycles—who is just as involved in destruction as in construction? How does that idea affect your interest in knowing God? Is it a pull toward or a push away?

Notes

1. Stephen King, *Storm of the Century: The Labor Day Hurricane of 1935* (New York: Simon & Schuster, 1999), 272.

2. Cameron Harder, *The Shame of Farm Bankruptcy: A Sociological and Theological Investigation of Its Effect on Rural Communities*, PhD dissertation (Toronto: University of St. Michael's College, 1999).

3. Wikipedia, s.v. "Prosperity Theology," accessed July 16, 2019, https://tinyurl.com/oe3j6tz.

4. See the comprehensive study on the adherents of the prosperity gospel by Bradley Koch, "Who Are the Prosperity Gospel Adherents?" *Journal of Ideology* 36, no. 1 (2014), 21–24, accessed July 17, 2019.

5. See the online news stories at https://www.cbsnews.com/news/senate-panel-probes-6-top-televangelists/ and https://tinyurl.com/yj222zrf, accessed August 2, 2019.

6. Lindsay Elizabeth, "Beth Moore: Christians Who Proudly Reject the 'Prosperity Gospel' Are Embracing the 'Pampering Gospel,'" *Faithwire*, April 8, 2018, https://tinyurl.com/yfnrhznq.

7. Used by permission of Man Martin. See his cartoons at https://tinyurl.com/ydzfyu62.

8. In Hebrew, "Adam" means "of the earth" or "from the soil."

9. Abdu'l-Baha, "Beauty and Harmony in Diversity," *Paris Talks*, October 28, 1972, https://tinyurl.com/m5vqroh.

10. In 1948 Abraham Maslow developed his famous "hierarchy" of needs, which insists that humans will attend to basic physical and safety needs before social, emotional (self-esteem), and finally "self-actualization" needs. But as many authors have pointed out, basic

needs can only be met in cohesive communities where the social glue is strong, and the community has a sense of purpose and self-esteem. People connected to well-bonded communities will risk their lives for the sake of deeply held principles or for loved ones. See for example Pamela Rutledge's article "Social Networks: What Maslow Misses," *Psychology Today,* November 8, 2011, https://tinyurl.com/yefp9ns3.

11. Note that by "power" I don't just mean political power but all the ways in which people can influence others to get what they want, through money, gender, race, education/intelligence, charm/social skills, occupation, family position, and so on.

12. C. S. Lewis, *A Grief Observed* (New York: Seabury, 1961).

13. Douglas John Hall, *God and Human Suffering: An Exercise in the Theology of the Cross* (Minneapolis: Fortress Press, 1986).

14. C. S. Lewis, *Till We Have Faces: The Myth of Cupid and Psyche*, 2nd ed., e-artnow, 2016, p. 131.

8

How Do We Choose a "Good" Religion?

If you don't belong to a particular faith community, you may be interested in a research project I carried out in 2014. I visited Christian ministries in western Canada that were making strong connections with Canadians. I asked these new folks why they became interested in these ministries. In a nutshell, they told me they'd found a place of grace that would nurture their spirit, help them build supportive friendships with other people, and assist them in living their work and family lives with more integrity. Here are a few quotes from those interviews to give you a taste of their responses:

- "I didn't grow up in church. But I like the underlying message here—acceptance, open doors, breaking barriers down, open communication. The preconceived notions I had about church have been pushed aside. At first, I was nervous that they would try to convert me. You never know how religious people are going to respond to you—I'm an outsider. You don't know if they're going to judge you. . . . I didn't want to feel pressured."

- "I wanted to sit down and participate in conversation, not be talked or lectured to."

- "I don't think our spiritual and physical life are that different—they go hand in hand. I work at a local financial institution. And I find a lot of that spiritual knowledge fits into my dealings with my customers. You don't leave your spirituality at the church door when you walk into the world."

- "God to me is working every second of every day in all of our lives in all of our sacred spaces."

- "[These church folks] share love in an easy way."

- "It wasn't a scary place—it wasn't rigid. . . . It's a fairly safe environment to express ourselves."

- "It's so lovely that they welcome me into their homes and are so kind."

- "[In this faith group] we've opened up more deeply, more quickly. . . . There's an atmosphere of safety."

- "People are having fun, supporting each other, interacting with people they normally wouldn't interact with."

- "This is fun—sitting around, talking freely, not necessarily following a script."

- "It gives me grounding, a base of support, that I can approach anyone in the group. It gives me stability, so I don't have nothing to refer to or get help. That's why we started going—to have a support system for the family to have."

Not everyone, of course, is looking for the same thing when they connect with a faith community. Each person's country of origin, family background, and personal experiences with religion will shape their particular needs.

Below are five criteria that I would use to find a suitable faith group. They reflect my own bias that the community be sustainable and life-affirming. The last criterion—"openness"—is particularly useful in revealing this, so I have provided some concrete questions/suggestions for assessing openness.

1. Is the Religion Modest about Its Truth Claims?

As a pastor and professor, I have frequently been asked "Which religion has *the truth*?" I usually reply "Most *claim* to. *None* do. And if any religion actually did have 'the whole truth and nothing but the truth,' it would be *useless* to us."

The reason it would be useless is the self-evident fact (to some at least) that we are not gods. We can't grasp *truth* or *reality* in all its extraordinary complexity. There is an immense amount of information bombarding us every moment. Our brains just can't process the vast flow of data that even our local reality supplies. We're like a minnow trying to swallow the mighty Mississippi!

So our brain dumbs it down. Several times in this book, I have referred to religions as "apps"—simplifications of reality that allow us to interface with spiritual matters in a useful way. That comparison is based on the work of Donald Hoffman, professor of cognitive sciences at the University of California. Hoffman and his team have discovered that in computer simulations of evolution, those organisms that knew *too much* about their environment didn't survive.[1] The ones that were most successful developed "life hacks"—simple and effective rules, habits, perspectives—that made them better competitors for scarce resources. TMI (too much information) bogged them down.

To explain, Hoffman compares human perception of reality to a computer screen. The screen does not show us the *reality* of the computer—its diodes, resisters, electron movements, and megabytes of memory. If you had to deal with all that, you could never go online, read your email, check your bank account, or play a game. In fact, what the computer screen shows us is *nothing* like the inside of a computer. The screen *hides* reality, so we can do real things on the computer.

Our brain's perceptual systems work like that too—by *concealing in a useful way*, they give us a reality we can handle. Our brains create, for example, a simple image of a banana out of the torrent of electromagnetic waves striking our retina, so we can recognize food and eat it. Gravitational waves from every mass in the universe pass through us, those from our earth being strong enough to jostle the crystals in our inner ear. Our brain simplifies it to "up and down," enabling us to stand upright.

Human community does something similar. It creates a *culture*—a network of behaviors, beliefs, symbols, and social institutions—that simplifies reality for us, so we can interact with it effectively. Religions are an aspect of that cultural interface (I've been calling them "God-user-interfaces" or "GUIs"[2]). These GUIs help us find meaning in life and navigate the turbulent waters of complex relationships between people, the land, and God. Through rituals, stories, and common habits of life, they build an image (to use theologian Hans Frei's term[3]) of "a habitable world"—a world in which we can live *well*. That image does *not* show us what God-Reality is *actually* like—we couldn't comprehend it if it did. But if the religious GUI is well designed, it allows us to *interact* with God-Reality in a way that meets human needs and matches our limited abilities.

2. Does the Religion Actually Work?

Like computer apps, religious truth claims can be assessed to some degree by how well they do what they are intended to do. If I buy a word-processing app and find out that it has no printing option or no spell-checker and posts my private banking files to Facebook when I hit the $ sign, I'd have to say its claim to be a word-processing app is false. Malware in fact! But if I learn the app, use it properly, and find that it helps me write a blog, prepare a college research paper, or write legible minutes for a committee meeting—then I'd conclude its claim is true.

In the same way, religions can be judged by how well they "work." Of course, like computer apps, not all religions have the same purpose. Some may be designed to appease ever-vigilant deceased ancestors, others to ensure that one gets to a "good place" after they die. Whether or not *those* religions "work" may be impossible to assess since—to most people at least—the post-death realm isn't accessible.

Other spiritual traditions however focus more on *this* life. Some—like Confucianism or Buddhism—are not concerned so much with God as with human development.[4] They are wisdom traditions (like the book of Proverbs in the Hebrew/Christian scriptures) that guide people toward a life that is peaceful, enlightened, self-controlled, or conflict-free. It's somewhat easier in such cases to tell whether the tradition is working for its adherents.

Be aware that a religious group's *expressed* aims may differ from its *real* but hidden purpose. Some computer apps look benign but actually are *designed* to be destructive, harboring trojan horses, ransomware, or worms. Similarly, religious "cults" occasionally form around a charismatic leader who claims that he wants to provide his followers with a special experience of God but who actually wants to control their lives or gain sexual favors.

Clearly, a religious app that harbors such a virus can't be treated as *true;* it doesn't do what it publicly claims, and what it *does* do is destructive.

Personally, I assess the truth of religious beliefs and practices by how they affect a community. If they link members together in a web of healthy relationships, if they foster the development of people who are open to God, open to the neighbor, and open to the future, I regard it as grounded in something true. Doesn't matter if its stories are more myth than history and its rituals a bit bizarre.

On the other hand, if the practices of a religion work only for its leaders and not for its people, if they concentrate power in a few and disempower the rest—in other words, if they don't work to build healthy people and healthy communities—I would judge their claims to be false. The prosperity gospel mentioned in a previous chapter is an example of the latter.

3. Do Members Take Their Religion Seriously?

Even a well-designed computer app won't work well, of course, if it's not *used* properly. With religious GUIs too, proper use is key. By "proper use" I mean that a religious tradition will work for a community only if: (1) it takes the tradition *seriously*, and (2) if it doesn't take its tradition *too* seriously.

To "take a religion seriously" means engaging it *as if* the world the religion describes is real . . . even though we know it is just a *constructed interface* with reality, like a computer app. Now this might sound hypocritical. But it's the same thing we do with computers. If I download an app that claims to be a word-processing program, I don't expect it to reveal to me the secret circuits of the computer's motherboard. I treat its tools and screens *as if* what they present to me is real.

A few years ago, I interviewed people in Alberta's oil industry to see how (if) their faith affected their work. I spent time with barons of the industry in Calgary towers, with landowners in farm country, and with workers in the oil sands. Each time I asked them, "What effect does your faith tradition have on the way you view and do your work in the oil patch?"

Some talked about how their spiritual tradition helped them in their relationships with other workers. A couple saw their work in the Alberta oil sands as a way of tending God's creation by cleaning up a "natural disaster." But many of them had great difficulty identifying any connection at all between their work and their faith. One who had been an active churchgoer their whole life said, "What we talk about on Sunday and what I do at work on Monday are two different things. There's no relationship between them." The comment was discouraging for me.

And then I interviewed a Muslim man who was an executive in one of the larger oil-sands projects. He gave me example after example of how stories and principles from the Qur'an have shaped the way he approaches his work. I was quite impressed and asked him how he was able to make those connections so easily. "Two simple things," he said. "First, when I was young, I had to memorize the Qur'an, word for word. It's in my head. Second, three times during my workday, I follow the Muslim practice of taking time out for prayer. I find that as I pray, the presence of God and those Qur'anic stories tucked away in my head begin to frame what's happening in my workday. I often come out of prayer with a new perspective on a business decision." That Muslim took faith *seriously*, learning his tradition thoroughly, practicing it rigorously.

My Muslim friend was able to make significant faith–work life connections because he took the Qur'an seriously. But that's not easy. All sacred texts are rife with contradictions and perplexing statements. In part, this is due to the variety of editors and sources that inevitably influence long-lived texts. But the contradictions should not be easily dismissed. As Niels Bohr, the Nobel-winning physicist once said, "The opposite of a true statement is a false statement, but the opposite of a profound truth can be another profound truth."[5]

In fact, much of life is lived between opposing truths. For example, a mother says to her daughter one day, "I love you." The next day she says, "Go to your room and take a time out!" To the child, the second statement contradicts the first. But the mother knows that there is a deeper connection—that loving her daughter means helping her daughter learn self-control.

Sacred texts are full of such paradoxes. In the Christian Bible we are told: God is one (Mark 12:29), but God is three—Father, Son, and Holy Spirit (Matt 28:19); all will be saved (1 Cor 15:22) but some will be damned (John 3:18); children will suffer for the sins of their parents (Exod 20:5) but they should *not* be punished for the sins of their parents (Deut 24:16). Or in the Qur'an: God forgives all sins (39:53) but will not forgive some sins (47:34; 9:80); humans are created out of water (24:45) or semen (16:4) or clay (6:2); drinking alcohol is good nourishment (16:66–67) but a great sin (2:219) and Satan's handiwork (5:90–91). And so on.

Faced with such bewildering contradictions, it's easy to set ancient texts aside. But I prefer to see them as a spiritual *gymnasium*. If a religion takes its texts seriously, it means its members have to wrestle with *both* sides of its paradoxes. In the process they develop spiritual insight. They learn how to see things from different perspectives. They build moral muscles, learning how to make ethical decisions when faced with tough choices. They gain wisdom as they notice the polar tensions of their own lives mirrored in the texts—hope and lament, fear and love, revenge and forgiveness—and can see how others have dealt with them.

Even if a religion "works," you might protest that believing "as if" is a tough feat of mental gymnastics when so many of its elements seem fantastical: "How can I pray to a God that looks like a Buddha-elephant (Ganesh) or a three-headed hydra (the Trinity)? It's ridiculous!" Well, not necessarily. I took a college class in the anatomy of pain back in the '70s. At that time scientists rejected acupuncture as a legitimate therapy because it was couched in the language of Hindu/Buddhist mysticism, referring to the unblocking of "chakras" and flows of spiritual energy. It seemed weird and "New Agey" to me too. Nonetheless, I and medical scientists have since discovered that acupuncture *works*. I have watched friends and family go through the procedure and had it myself. Even knowing that the language used by the therapist was symbolic, acupuncture brought us significant pain relief. Since then, medical practitioners have replaced chakra talk with reference to "nerve centers" (the language of *science's* virtual reality), and acupuncture is now widely accepted.

Faith is like that too. It doesn't mean jettisoning our brains, but it does mean understanding the limits of human perception and sometimes surrendering to a kind of "informed foolishness." We can never deal directly with the forces of the universe in their elemental state. All we can *ever* work with, from bodily sensations to religious convictions, are symbols and metaphors that help us engage those forces in a life-giving way. So, the question for religion is, are the symbols we are using *effective*? Are they doing what we hope they're doing? Are they nurturing life or spreading death? How are they *actually* functioning?

4. Does the Religion "Update Its Apps"?

Not surprisingly, elements in a religious tradition change in meaning over time. Stories don't have the same impact in one generation or culture as they do in another. So, just as good computer apps are constantly evolving, religious language and ritual need to be *continually updated* to be effective.

The problem is that sometimes our religious apps get stuck,

frozen in time. Most often, it's because users take them *too* seriously; they don't realize their religion *is* an app. Often leaders who have expertise and authority in a particular religious tradition don't want it to change, because then they will lose their "expert" status. So subtly, or explicitly, they may claim that the current expression of their faith is "*The Truth*" in an absolute sense. To update, they say, would be equivalent to forsaking the truth, even forsaking God. It would be to engage in blasphemy and heresy, with accompanying eternal consequences.

What leaders like these are really doing is fostering idolatry. In my tradition, Martin Luther spoke of creation as God's "mask." He said we can engage God only through that mask, through stories and rituals that make use of the ordinary stuff of creation—bread and wine, land and water, plants, animals, people, and events. If we take hold of these natural elements in the awareness that God is fully present in them (as in all things), they can be a "means" or conduit of God's grace for us. But just because we take these physical and social and symbolic elements *seriously* does not mean that we can *identify* them with God. To let them *become* God for us is idolatry.

Yet, I'm afraid this happens often. A religion's sacred texts, ancient rituals, treasured images, or specially worded beliefs may be very useful in certain contexts. But the moment they become unalterable, the moment they take the place of God, these grace conduits get plugged up. The religion bogs down in a useless, even toxic, idolatry. It can no longer mediate to a changing community the Divine presence hidden deep inside. Its God-user-interface needs updating!

An example of a failure to update

Let me share an example from my own Christian tradition. I grew up being told that Jesus was tortured to death on a Roman cross because God had a problem: God was so angry with us for being disobedient that God wanted to kill us and then torture us forever in hell after we died. However, God somehow also loved us and deep down didn't want to do those horrible things to us. Unfortunately, God was compelled (by some unspecified universal law greater than God?) to *kill something* to purge all that anger and balance the books. God's solution to the dilemma was to take out the Divine wrath on his Son Jesus instead, making sure that Jesus died a protracted, painful death in our place. (It wasn't always clear whether Jesus *volunteered* to be God's victim or was *assigned* the role.)

Of course, our teachers never stated things quite this baldly, but that was the gist of the teaching, and it showed up frequently in sermons, hymns, and rituals. And to be honest, in some ways the story worked in our community. We felt that because of Jesus's sacrifice, God was on our side now and wouldn't get angry with us again. That brought a measure of freedom from guilt, a sense that there could be new beginnings after a failure.

But over time I became uneasy with this story. It seemed to portray God much like an abusive parent with anger control issues. And that's not an image our church normally endorses. A couple of incidents caused me to thoroughly rethink it.

First, a woman who had visited our church in Calgary came to me after the worship service in tears. Pointing to the crucifix at the front she said, "Whenever I see Jesus up on the cross like that, I just identify so much with him. Growing up, I had a sociopathic father like Jesus did, one who sacrificed us children to his own purposes. My dad always said he had good reasons for what he did, but *we* were the ones who suffered."

The second incident took place after 9/11. Our seminary study conference focused on Islam, and we decided to find out more about Muslims by visiting the local mosque. After a tour and some explanations, we gathered in a room for coffee and discussion. One of our members asked (quite rudely, I thought), "How can you folks say you're saved when you haven't got Jesus's blood to cover your sins?" One of the Muslim elders thought for a moment, then gently replied, "We don't think God has to *kill* something in order to forgive. God can simply forgive. We believe God is *merciful*. Don't you?" And then he went on, "Even if God did have to kill in order to forgive, God would never kill the *innocent* so the guilty could go free. We believe God is *just*. Don't you?" In that moment, I could feel in myself and see in the group of Christians (mostly clergy) around me, a kind of awakening: "Oh, this is what our beliefs look like to outsiders. . . . That's pretty horrible! Maybe we should rethink how Jesus's death saves us."

Turns out that this "atonement theory" app that makes Jesus the victim of an abusive heavenly Father is the result of a failure to update. It is a corrupted version of a doctrine developed at the end of the eleventh century CE by Anselm, an Italian monk in the Benedictine order of the Catholic Church.

Anselm lived in a medieval "honor and shame" monarchy. Using the language and thought forms of his day, he tried to explain to his people how Jesus's death helps us. He said that our sinful failure to obey God brings dishonor on God (the King). God's *reputation*—and thus the reputation of the whole kingdom of God—has been damaged by our disobedience. But that damage can't be undone by *us*. Even if we are obedient from now on, that can't make up for our prior sins, because obedience is *expected*. The insult God has suffered can only be restored by the gift of something that *isn't* required. Since Jesus had not sinned and did not deserve any punishment, he was able to step in and offer himself as a sacrifice. On behalf of all humanity, Jesus did *more* than was required, thus restoring God's honor.

Now, however well this theory may have worked in Anselm's day (and I'm not sure it did), it makes very little sense in our own time, at least in Western democracies that have social/political structures very different from Anselm's. Clearly, a theory about how God "saves" us that is based on medieval monarchy and redemptive sacrifice needs updating. It's interesting that there are examples of such an overhaul in some of the early Hebrew scriptures. One of them is in Genesis 22. (I like this story because it is counterintuitive—the main point sneaks up on you.)

In Genesis chapter 22, God asks Abraham to sacrifice his only son Isaac—the son promised and long awaited to carry on Abraham's legacy. Now, later Hebrew scriptures strongly forbid religious child sacrifice (e.g., Lev 18:21; 20:2–5; 2 Kings 23:10; Jer 32:35; 1 Kings 11:7).[6] So imagine you are part of a Jewish community that knows these scriptures, and you're listening to the story. God is telling Abraham to sacrifice Isaac. What would you think? I'd be horrified! I'd be thinking, "Abraham, this is a *test*. God is playing 'devil's advocate.' He doesn't actually want you to do this abominable thing that others around you are doing. So, don't give in! *Argue* with God, just as you did when you protested the destruction of Sodom and Gomorrah. God provoked you to compassion then. Can you not show it for your own son?!" But Abraham passively does the unimaginable. He takes Isaac up on a mountain. He's preparing to stab and incinerate Isaac when God (perhaps with a deep sigh) intervenes and says, "Abraham—let your son go. I'll provide a ram to sacrifice." I think this story was included in the Hebrew scriptures to *end* a horrific religious practice.

An additional update is done by the prophet Micah, who casts doubt on the value of *any* kind of sacrifice:

> Will the Lord be pleased with thousands of rams, with ten thousand rivers of olive oil? Shall I give my firstborn for my transgression, the fruit of my body for the sin of my soul? He has told you, O mortal, what is good; and what does the Lord require of you but to do

justice, and to love kindness, and to walk humbly with your God. (Mic 6:7–8)

Is God offended by updates to our belief systems?

Some religions do claim that their sacred texts are unalterable, absolute truth based on a direct revelation from God. For example, the Qur'an, the Book of Mormon, the Hebrew and Christian scriptures are often viewed that way. But four things need to be said about this:

First, every "word from God" has been *mediated*. Initially someone brought it to the community and claimed, "This is what God says." In the case of the Qur'an, it was Muhammad. With the Book of Mormon, it was Joseph Smith, and with the books of the Bible, it was various prophets, poets, and authors.

But Muhammad couldn't record the angel Gabriel's voice. Smith didn't produce the golden plates on which the Book of Mormon was supposed to have been written. And no voice from heaven spoke to Jews and Christians to confirm the inspired nature of their biblical writings. So how do we know these words are *God's* and not just the vacuous pronouncements of people with big egos trying to claim God's support for their personal project? Well, in each case a community has had to *decide:* "Can we trust this person? Did they actually hear God or are they deluded? Does what they say ring true with our experience of God and the world? Does it make our lives better? Does it *work?*"

Determining what is or isn't "God's word" has always been a pragmatic communal task. If I were God, I would be glad (even insist!) that my people exercise that sort of critical thinking when someone claims to speak for me (which, you must admit, is a pretty presumptuous thing to do!).

Second, though I can't really know God's mind, it seems consistent that the One who created an evolving universe that is constantly experimenting with new forms and discarding those that are no longer sustainable would be in favor of updating its religions. And I would expect that any communication from such a Creator would be *current*, a "Word of God" for *us, now*, in the world we live in today—not simply a reiteration of a revelation given to ancestors centuries ago on the other side of the earth.

Third, no matter what they claim, every religion *already has* a history of updates, and the change agents usually attribute the updates to Divine inspiration. The Bible, for example, is a library of oral stories, community policies, genealogies, songs, and so on that were told, written down, collated, edited, and translated over several centuries. Each item had its own original audience, its own time-and-culture-bound context. Later communities of faith chose which of the materials passed on to them best reflected their experience of God, and they modified those materials, often adding new ones of their own. As a result, today the Bibles of Eastern Orthodox Christians do not have the same books as those of Roman Catholic Christians, and their list is different from that of Pentecostal Christians.[7]

Similarly, Hinduism's most ancient sacred texts, the Vedas (composed prior to 800 BCE), were modified and reinterpreted by the authors of the Upanishads (composed 800 to 500 BCE). As in the Protestant Reformation and Pietist traditions in Christianity, the Upanishads called for a return to a more personal and meditative faith, in contrast to the formal, ritualized religion of early Hinduism. And there are other writings too—the Bhagavad Gita and other Hindu epics, the poetry of the Puranas, and so on—that have gained prominence over the centuries as Hindu communities have struggled to fit their faith to changing circumstances. Religious evolution of this sort is inevitable because communities flourish when their religion is *bespoke*—custom-fitted to their unique needs.

Finally—and this may be the real challenge for religion in the twenty-first century—community needs are morphing so rapidly that religions can't update fast enough, even if they are determined to do so. Every culture is being inundated by cultural products from many others (especially from the US). Through global media, powerful new ideas are streamed directly into the homes of even the most isolated communities every day. Words change meanings. Values shift. Symbols morph. Religious organizations that are stiffly resistant to change can place their adherents under tremendous stress as they force people to choose between the traditions of their faith community and the rapidly changing realities of twenty-first-century life.

Of course, it's not surprising that religious organizations are cautious about change. Historically, the update of a religious app has often led to a split in the community, for example between Jews and Christians; Catholic, Orthodox, and Protestant Christians; Sunni and Shiite Muslims; Hindus, Buddhists, and Sikhs; and so on. Too often that separation has been accompanied by violent conflict. So perhaps it's understandable that leaders are prone to frame new developments as "heresy" or "apostasy" (forsaking the faith).

But the globalization of religion does not have to spawn constant conflict. Religious leaders can remember that the God they worship in their churches/temples/mosques is the same God who loves and inhabits the changing world around them, with *all* its religious expressions. If they taught their children from birth that faith is an ongoing spiritual "experiment" with God, rather than just the guarding of an ancient treasure, perhaps faith updates would come to be seen as a normal—if often challenging and frustrating—part of religious life just as it is in our digital world.

5. Is the Religion Open to God, the Neighbor, and the Future?

All biological systems, including human systems are, by nature, *necessarily* open. That means that there are an enormous number of options available for their evolution. It also means that it is impossible to fully control that development.

When I talk about the "openness" of a religious community, I don't mean to imply that there is such a thing as a truly "closed" community. Rather I am referring to the organization's *level of comfort* with its unavoidable openness. Does the community embrace the uncertain, experimental quality of its life, or is it spending a lot of energy trying to control, fence it in? If the latter, then that energy won't be available for ministry or its own growth.

An example: one church building in which I worked had many doors because it had grown by absorbing or linking to other nearby buildings. As a result, security was very difficult. The building was *inherently* vulnerable. But, not able to accept that, our staff spent large amounts of staff meeting time trying to control keys and access. Energy that should have been spent on reaching out to the community was vainly spent on trying to keep it out.

Following are three aspects of openness that a religious organization may embrace or resist.[8] The questions that follow are intended to help someone visiting or researching the community to do a quick assessment of them.

Openness to God

- Who prays? Is it only trained leaders who pray out loud in public or in small groups, or is everyone encouraged to develop confidence in talking to God?

- Who is visibly "in contact" with God? Of course, if God is *everywhere*, then *everyone* is in constant contact with God, whether they know it or not. But is that the impression you get? Is everyone encouraged to share their ideas about, and experiences of, God (perhaps in large gatherings or small groups)? Or do you get the impression that God connects to this community only through a narrow pipeline from God to a key leader? Do members gather to wrestle with how to apply their faith to life in the workplace, home, and school? Or do they gather only to listen to a leader tell them who God is and what they should do?

- How diverse are the images of God used in worship, casual conversation, or public communications? Does the faith community draw on a wealth of metaphors and stories to express its experiences of God? Or is talk about God restricted to certain "right" phrases and metaphors?

- Do you pick up an emotional undertone of *gratitude* and *wonder*—a sense that God is all around, that the life of this community and of the world is in God's hands? Or is there an undertone of fear with constant reference to "forces of evil" or "the devil"?

- How are sacred writings handled? Is there an openness to God speaking *now*, not only in the past? Are new interpretations of scriptures allowed? Are all questions welcome, or are some questions out-of-bounds?

Openness to the Neighbor

- Whose stories are told in large gatherings, in the faith community's newsletter, or online media? Is it just the stories of prominent members? Or are the stories of the "weakest" members shared—stories of children, nondominant racial groups, the physically and mentally challenged, the sick, people of differing social status and sexual orientation, and people who belong to shame-based categories—those who have been in prison, have suffered rape, struggle with addiction, are unemployed or bankrupt, and so on?

- Who attends public gatherings of the faith community? To what extent do the colors of skin, vocal accents, and clothing styles reflect the range of these in the wider community outside? Is there special attention given to marginal groups, or does the faith community reflect mostly those who have power in the wider neighborhood?

- What is the emotional undertone you pick up regarding others? Is it one of acceptance, compassion for sufferers of any sort, vulnerability about one's faults and struggles, an atmosphere of *grace*?

- How is humor used? How seriously does the community take itself? Can it poke fun at itself? Do those who have power and authority poke fun at themselves? Or is *ridicule* used instead of humor and directed at people outside the faith community (especially other religions or people who are weak or marginal in some way)?

- What are the connections between this community and other communities of faith nearby or around the world (and not just of the same religious stripe)?

- How is this faith community in partnership with other local organizations to increase the well-being of the neighborhood?

- How is power used in the faith community? Are members *empowered* or *disempowered*? Is there training and ongoing support for volunteers? Do decision makers include in their planning the people who will be *most affected by* a decision?

Openness to the Future

- What is the emotional undertone of the gatherings? How often is the future spoken of fearfully? How often do you hear expressions of *hope*?

- Do you get the feeling that the future is open for this group, or does it feel like there are some "buried landmines," "skeletons in the closet," or painful past incidents that curb their willingness to consider options for the future?

- Do you get the impression that this is a learning community, wanting to grow into maturity? Does the community gather information about the *impact* its ministry is having on people, so the ministries can make adjustments? Do people talk as though life is a spiritual experiment undergirded by God's grace, or do you get the sense that there is one right way for most things and if people don't find it they are in trouble?

- Is the community free to fail? Are projects treated as "life-and-death," or is there a lightness about them, a spirit of adventure, a readiness to re-jig and try again, or try something else?

- Which is more prominent in the life of the community: promise or warning? Constant *warnings* (which I admit are *sometimes* necessary) imply that members are weak, immature children in the faith who need to be protected by "parental" figures. *Promises* imply that there is confidence in the members, that they are being encouraged to experiment, to take some risks, bolstered by God's presence and grace. Promises must not be empty, however, but based on real experience—a *grounded* trust in God.

Vulnerable but secure

Openness is great. But with openness comes *vulnerability*. All faith communities have members who are particularly at risk—children, elderly, those suffering from physical or mental illnesses, people with a history of abuse (physical, mental, spiritual). To be healthy, safe, and sustainable, a faith community can be truly open only if it is also *secure*. That means the group has:

1. *Careful leadership selection.* Key leaders will not normally volunteer for their position. They will be *recruited* by the community, which has noticed that they have the abilities a particular role requires and also have the humility, courage, and compassion to exercise it well.

2. *Strong systems of support and accountability* in place to ensure that the strong don't prey on the weak and that those who disclose their suffering will not have it used against them. This requires

    a. Clear *policies* for the protection of children, youth, the sick, and the frail elderly. See the resource materials in the chapter on child sexual abuse for examples.

    b. Well-used *feedback mechanisms* for key leaders to help them see how they are actually affecting the people they work with. This usually involves some confidential interviews of those whom key leaders have interacted with, by a team of non-leaders who have excellent listening skills.

c. *Training* for all key leaders, not only in their area of expertise, but also in how to oversee and support those they work with.

3. Explicit *processes for conflict resolution* that minimize collateral damage to folks not directly affected by the conflict but also ensure that complaints aren't suppressed and can be brought forward in an open manner to a disinterested party (i.e., someone who doesn't have a conflict of interest).

4. *Social glue:* that is, effective processes for building *bonds* between members, *bridges* between members and the wider community, and *links* between the organization and supervisory structures in the regional/national religious body. This would include a sufficiently extensive discipline for integrating new members into the community.

I know that it is not possible to get comprehensive information on all these matters without being involved in a community for a while. But keeping the questions in mind should help as you explore. Make the most of your time when you visit a worship service or event. Try to think like a sociologist. Observe carefully, write down your observations and impressions after the service, and talk them over with family and friends.

You can also get information from a group's website, which may contain worship bulletins, newsletters, and links to social media sites. These will be designed to impress of course, but they should offer some useful info.

In the end you will be left with some questions. I would suggest talking with a member who is relatively new to the group, another who has been there a long time, and a key leader. All of them may be interested in "recruiting" you to the group, and want to put the best face on things, so you'll have to be gently persistent in pressing more difficult questions.

Finally, if you are becoming seriously interested, I would talk to a few folks in the neighborhood who aren't involved with that organization. What kind of reputation does it have? How are its members engaged with other community groups?

If you find a place to put down roots, recognize that the group will change over time and, like all human institutions, have its share of the good, the bad, and the ugly. Patience, forgiveness, clear feedback, and trusting in God to work through flawed people will help you stay the course with them (and they with you!).

Explore!

1. Open Google Maps online and type in "religious organizations" in the search box. What do you notice about the variety (or lack) of religious groups in your area?

2. Visit two of the religious organizations whose websites interest you (best to go with a family member or friend for support). If you have been involved with a particular faith tradition for a long time, visit a couple of places that are different from yours. If you have not been religiously active, pick a couple of places whose programs and self-description resonate with you.

3. At the visits, be observant. Write down four or five of the questions in this chapter that people could ask if they were looking for a healthy faith community and

keep them in a pocket or purse. Try to collect answers to some of them about this faith community during the visit.

4. Debrief with your visit partner. How did you feel before, during, and after the visit? What attracted or intrigued you? What turned you off? What surprised you? What are you interested in following up on?

5. From your encounters with religion/religious people, what have you noticed that has been "updated" over the years? Do the updates seem to be helping? Why or why not?

Notes

1. Donald Hoffman, "Do we see reality as it is?" *TED Talks*, Youtube.com, accessed August 5, 2019, https://tinyurl.com/ngykz97.

2. As noted earlier "GUI" normally refers to "graphical-user-interface." Microsoft's Windows is an example, as are all visually based computer applications.

3. Hans Frei, *The Eclipse of Biblical Narrative: A Study in Eighteenth and Nineteenth Century Hermeneutics*, rev. ed. (New Haven: Yale University Press, 1980).

4. Note that most Buddhist traditions do not profess faith in a personal God, though some do. Generally, the focus is on reaching a state of "Nirvana"—complete peace through enlightenment.

5. Hans Bohr, "My Father," in *Niels Bohr: His Life and Work as Seen by His Friends and Colleagues* (Amsterdam: North-Holland, 1967), 328.

6. Klaas Smelik, "Moloch, Molekh or molk-sacrifice? A reassessment of the evidence concerning the Hebrew term Molekh," *Scandinavian Journal of the Old Testament* 9, no. 1 (1995); John Gee and Kerry Muhlestein, "An Egyptian Context for the Sacrifice of Abraham," *Journal of Book of Mormon Studies* 20, no. 2 (2011): Article 6,

accessed August 11, 2019, https://tinyurl.com/tp989mg.

7. Wikipedia has a nice visual description of the development of the biblical canon (list of books) in different traditions. S.v. "Biblical Canon," accessed August 13, 2019, https://tinyurl.com/mesnxnc.

8. I owe something of the original concept to Daniel Migliore, who uses these forms of openness as a way of describing what it means to be "made in the image of God." See his book *Faith Seeking Understanding*, 2nd ed. (Grand Rapids: Eerdmans, 2004).

9

Why I Am a Christian

I can't close this book without being honest about my own religious choices. As far back as I can remember, I have been interested in God. But I didn't make the rounds of world religions to see which suited me best. Nor did I compare religions online, read Google reviews, and make a rational selection. Like most of the world, I was simply born into a family and community already infused with religious traditions. My parents came from United Church of Canada (Christian liberal) and United Evangelical Brethren (Christian conservative) backgrounds. They decided to attend a local Lutheran mission as a compromise—and that's where I grew up. Their choice set the arena for my spiritual education. I was influenced by various pastors, Lutheran confirmation training, and eventually teachers and friends during two years in a Bible school. During university I decided that my deepest satisfaction for an adult career would be as a Christian pastor, helping people explore and grow in their faith. I didn't imagine any religious setting other than the one in which I'd grown up.

But just before I was to move myself and my family to Saskatoon for pastoral training, I had a moment of exceptional clarity.

It was the end of a long day's work. As I put down my tools and stared out over the northern Alberta fields, I felt a deep stillness inside, as if time were suspended. I saw that my life was at a crossroads—that no matter what spiritual tradition my community had given me, I wasn't bound by it; I had a real choice to make that would shape the course of my life. Later, I wrote down my impressions of that moment in diary form:

It's a summer evening. I'm standing on a dusty road in northern Alberta, watching the sun set, struggling with my future. "Do I really want to be a pastor?" I wonder. "What do I know of God? What if it's all make-believe? How can I spend my life asking people to put their trust in a God I've never seen?"

I guess I'm looking for proof, for a sign. But God doesn't give me one. At least, no handwriting in the sky, no burning bush, no angel visitation. Instead God gives me a Person. Images of Jesus, as I imagined him in the gospel stories I've heard since childhood, flash through my mind:

Jesus is walking barefoot down the beach of Galilee's sea, the wind in his hair. He strolls past the nets of Peter and Andrew. With a strange joy in his eyes, Jesus invites them to come, let go of nets and security and even life. And they do. What kind of man is this?

Jesus is in the grain field with his new friends. It's the Sabbath and food can't be gathered without incurring the anger of the Sabbath-keepers. But Jesus harvests to feed his companions anyway. And when the food-police come he takes the flak.

Jesus is kneeling in the streets of Capernaum among the lepers and the lame, touching their hearts with hope, touching their bodies with health. He touches and is rendered unclean by them, but they are infected by his life, and made well.

Jesus is asleep in a boat during a violent storm on the Sea of Galilee. The disciples are bailing like mad, scared to death; they have forgotten that God is in their boat. Jesus reminds them by standing up in the teeth of that gale. Lashed by wind and spray, he speaks to the wild elements in a voice that comes from the dawn of time—"Be still!" and Chaos submits.

Jesus stands outside Gerasa, near the place of a Roman massacre. He confronts the Legion of evil spirits that inspired the horrors done there by the Roman military legion. For the sake of one demon-tormented man he dares to challenge the tyrants of darkness. And they retreat.

Jesus talks theology with a woman—a Syrophoenician, no less! It's unheard of for those times—the Son of God debating theology with a Gentile woman. And he concedes the debate to her! Jesus loses face so that she might be lifted from social disgrace. Who is this, I wondered, who cares about the honor of others, especially the dishonored, more than his own? Why doesn't he pander to status and power? He seems true to himself no matter who he is with.

I recall that Jesus is often with *outsiders*—hookers, tax collectors, the poor. He seems to have a special love for them. Perhaps that's why he gets so angry in the temple. He throws over the tables, shutting down the temple trade. The center of Jewish faith has become a money factory for Israel's elite. The poor, the sick, women and strangers are labelled "unclean" and have to buy their way out of shame at the temple vendors. Jesus steps into the gears of that unholy machine and grinds it to a halt. Ultimately, he loses his life in its teeth. But the unclean find theirs.

I remember that Jesus didn't have to die. He had a choice, right at the start—in the desert. The prince of darkness offered him the kingdoms of the world—the easy way—but Jesus wasn't interested in power and glory. And again at the end, before his arrest in the Garden of Gethsemane, in anguish over the cruel death before him, believing that angelic armies would protect him if he asked, Jesus refuses both fight and flight. He won't abandon his people and he won't summon violence to save himself.

So, in Herod's court, Jesus is silent. He doesn't play the games of his power-blinded captors. His eyes fill with pity as soldiers strip him, jam plaited thorns on his head and mock him.

Then that Beloved One, whose outstretched hands commanded seas and embraced children, stretches them out again to be pierced by cruel nails. In deep pain, he looks into the face of his executioners to say, "Father, forgive them, they don't know what they are doing."

And I realize: this one is truly worth dying for—yet he chooses to die a shameful, agonizing death for those who hate him.

That's why I follow Jesus, the Christ. Not because I'm a religious person, looking for a spiritual high. I'm a Christian because in Jesus I meet a Love that is more than human, a Love worth living for. That crucified and risen Christ parts the veil over God's face, and opens for me a life that death cannot crush.

Looking into that sunset, I realize that whatever doubts I might have, my life is not really my own. It already belongs to Jesus. I have never known anyone like him. So even if I never hear an angel's voice, or see a miracle, I will count my life worth something if I reach the end of my life and can say that in some feeble way I have known Jesus and followed him.

Decades after I wrote this, I am still captivated by Jesus. He has given me a compelling glimpse into who God is and what it means to be fully human. Jesus is *unique*.

Now I know that can also be truly said of Muhammad, the Buddha, and many others. Always, over the centuries, there have been people who have made the Creator's life visible in their communities in their own remarkable way. Using the analogy from an earlier chapter, they are like volcanoes that spill out into ordinary life the fiery hidden spirit of our planet. In the life of these women and men, the God who is just under the surface of all creation erupts into view.

So why do I stick with *Jesus*-shaped faith? First, because he captured my imagination and my heart early on. Since I can live on the slopes of only *one* "volcano" (though I can visit others and learn from them), I have decided to keep my home in the shadow of the one named Jesus.

Second, I have discovered over the years that Jesus's way of being in the world *works*. That's not to say that other spiritual traditions don't work. In fact, it seems likely that if people stick with a religion for centuries, that's because it meets a real human need. Nor am I saying that folks who name themselves "Christian" (i.e., followers of Jesus, the Christ) are better than the rest. Too often the things Christians say and do make it seem that they've never met the Jesus of the Bible (I've said a lot about that in this book!). But I *have* discovered that some dynamics of Jesus's life are really important for healthy human relationships and vital, sustainable communities. Following are some of those dynamics.

Jesus Builds Communities around the Weak

The Jesus we see in the Bible is certainly not a superman. Like every human, he eats, drinks, sleeps. He gets angry, tired, sad, excited, and frightened. He bleeds. He dies, just like the rest of us.

Jesus is born poor, conceived out of wedlock to peasant Jewish parents. But this isn't a poor-boy-makes-good story. Joseph, his dad, trains him to be a carpenter, but not long after Joseph dies, Jesus abandons that decent occupation to become an itinerant preacher, living off the generosity of women like Mary and Martha. And he encourages others to leave their jobs and follow him.

When Jesus *has* a chance at political power and wealth—offered to him by the Devil in the desert, or by crowds after he'd performed a miraculous "sign"—he rejects them. Jesus chooses to live in mutual dependence—or *interdependence*—rather than to secure his own life independently.

Similarly, Jesus rejects social power—the idea that you will be secure if others approve of you and serve you. So, when his friends get starry-eyed and ask to sit at Jesus's right hand when he comes into his power, Jesus sharply upbraids them:

> You know that those who are regarded as rulers of the Gentiles lord it over them, and their high officials exercise authority over them. Not so with you. Instead, whoever wants to become great among you must be your servant, and whoever wants to be first must be slave of all. (Mark 10:42–44)

Another time Jesus's friends ask him who is the "greatest" in God's kingdom. Jesus calls over a child and says to his friends, "Unless you change your attitudes and become like little children you will never enter the reign of God. Whoever humbles themselves like this little child is truly the greatest in the reign of God" (Matt 18:1–4).

In fact, many of the people Jesus chose to be his closest friends had little more status than children in their society. They were lepers, prostitutes, despised Roman tax collectors, fishers, the homeless and unemployed. One would have to agree when St. Paul says to the early Christians:

> Consider your own call, brothers and sisters: not many of you were wise by human standards, not many were powerful, not many were of noble birth. But God chose what is foolish in the world to shame the wise; God chose what is weak in the world to shame the strong; God chose what is low and despised in the world, things that are not, to reduce to nothing things that are, so that no one might boast in the presence of God. (1 Cor 1:26–29)

"God has *chosen* the *weak*." That's not what we normally hear—from parents, schoolteachers, or our Western media. The chosen, they tell us, are the smart, the strong, the sexy, the wealthy, and the driven; these are the ones who make the world go round.

But I have discovered that isn't true. Doing extensive research into rural communities, I have found that only communities that gather around their *weak* ones—the young, the sufferers, the frail elderly, the bankrupt—ultimately survive. For example, if they take children's needs seriously, the children become the heart of a network of caregivers—daycare providers, teachers, coaches, and so on. Looking after children, the adults of the community build friendships and economic links with *each other*. The structure of the whole community gets stronger. And young families come back to the town because they know their children will be cared for.

It's similar with those who go bankrupt. They are the ones who have fallen into a pothole on the economic road. If they are shunned or ignored by the community, then no one knows exactly where those potholes are. Many more fall in. But when those who lose their farms or businesses are supported and listened to, the community picks up on an injustice in local lending practices or an attitude that should be discouraged (e.g., new equipment is a sign of prosperity). Everyone is wiser.

Again, when those who have mental illnesses are cared for, the rest of the community is much more likely to go for help early when they start to feel depressed. Or when the frail elderly are visited, the community learns its own history and can make better decisions for its future. When victims and offenders are dealt with directly (rather than simply shipped over to prison warehouses), the whole community learns how to do reconciliation and restoration.

There are two keys to the power of the weak. The first, that I have harped on extensively, is that it undermines our human and religious tendency to see ourselves as little gods. The weak *know* they are not. As a result, they are less likely, for example, to see themselves as "stewards of creation" trying (often with disastrous results) to manage the vast, complex ecosystems of our planet. Not owning land and powerful technologies, the weak more easily recognize that we are one species among many and that our first task is simply to look after our own niche and maintain good neighborly relations with the others.

The second key is that the weak *need* others and they know it; they're not lone rangers. You can't build a community out of lone rangers, any more than you can build a Lego project with bricks that have bumps on all sides but no indentations. It's only when one person's weakness connects with another's strength that a bond can be formed.

In addition, when God does something extraordinary through a weak person (like Jesus, like his friends, like us), people often take it as a sign that *God* is at work. They may be surprised, but few are likely to be envious or resentful. Instead it's cause for hope: "If God can work through that poor soul, maybe God can work through me too!" Paul expresses this well in 2 Corinthians

4:7. "We have this treasure [the ministry of sharing what Jesus shows us of God] in *weak vessels* so that all can see that the power comes from God, and not from us" (author's translation).

As God works through the weak, a community learns to put its confidence not in one or two charismatic leaders or in the promises of a government or corporation (they inevitably disappoint), but in *God*, working through *everyone*.

A community built around the weak turns out to be more robust and resilient than one in which only the strong are honored. In fact, I found that communities that adopt a "survival of the fittest" mentality during times of intense stress often end up losing members rapidly. Schools, stores, and churches close; health facilities shut down.

One community that I visited in northern Alberta ended up with one landowner farming almost forty square miles of land. The hotel, general store, and a variety of other services had all been lost as one farmer after another had been forced or enticed out of business by this aggressive landowner, until only he was left. His "success" killed the community. Truth is, "survival of the fittest" is an *extinction* philosophy. And Jesus knew it.

Jesus Lives by Grace

Jesus's friends were a motley crew. As I noted, many came from the lowest rungs of his society. But some too were wealthy and well educated. Jesus befriended them all. His *indiscriminate* choice of companions highlights another principle that has turned out to be critically important in community health: that is, that a person's intrinsic "value" is determined by the Creator, not by oneself or others. So it can't be marred by failure. It can't be increased by income or achievement. It can't be polished by praise or sullied by censure.

What then is our value? Well, if all of creation is saturated by God's Spirit (and it's hard to imagine a universe that could exist without the Creator's sustaining presence *everywhere*), then everyone, everything, is a vessel for the Divine presence. That we are housed and inhabited by the Creator suggests that we are worth more to God than we can imagine.

Christian thinkers have called it "grace." Grace is God's *unearned* love and favor for all of humanity, for all of creation in fact. Grace-based faith insists that no matter how I feel about myself, or how other people regard me, no matter what I do or fail to do, my self-worth is *secure*. It's locked away in the heart of God. That is also true of the people and the Land around me. Whole communities, which have their own corporate identity and self-image, have that same God-given value that can't be lost.

I've discovered, as the old hymn claims, that grace *is* amazing. An encounter with grace can transform relationships. Let me give you a few examples based on my own experience:

1. Angela is thirteen. She struggles with self-esteem. Her friends are important, so she connects with them daily on social media. However, sometimes they ridicule or bully her online. That hurts a lot and hooks into her negative self-image. But then Angela's faith kicks in. She remembers what her mom has always told her: that despite how she feels, regardless of what others say, she is and always will be God's beloved. So, Angela blocks the bullies, reminds herself not to bully them back (for they are beloved too), and gets on with life.

2. Xiulan is a new Canadian and the first Asian to be elected in her electoral district. She knows she will be under intense scrutiny and is quite intimidated. Xiulan feels she *has* to succeed. So, as she responds to constituents' concerns, Xiulan's first impulse is to protect herself, to hide her inexperience and cover up when her

policies turn out to be unhelpful. But Xiulan's church friends remind her that she's free to fail; it won't change the honor she has in God's eyes. Tentatively exercising her confidence in God's grace, Xiulan slowly becomes able to ask for mentoring from experienced colleagues and to receive—even solicit—critical feedback nondefensively. As a result, she is able to respond much more effectively to the needs of her constituency.

3. Tom, a successful businessman, retires at sixty-five. All his life he has been measured by his income and the growth of his tech company. Now the business has been sold. Old colleagues don't call anymore. Tom feels that he has rolled off onto a social side-track. He misses the prestige his job gave him, and he doesn't know what to do with himself. Tom's not sure who he is anymore. Depression starts to settle in. But then Tom's priest takes him out for coffee. She reminds Tom that he is the same person he's always been—honored and loved by God; that hasn't changed. Tom believes her. It isn't easy, but Tom slowly begins to let go of the self the business world had constructed for him. He finds joy in exploring new relationships that are built on mutual interests and service.

4. Henry is in prison for armed robbery. He'd stolen things since he was young—got a buzz from the danger, from getting away with it. But he'd been caught by a security camera breaking into an upper-class home. And he was carrying a knife. So, he's in for two years. Some of the guards in the prison and most of the other prisoners treat Henry like crap. Henry just holes up in his cell, trying to do his time without too much hassle. Then the prison chaplain comes to visit. He

treats Henry with respect, doesn't grill him about his past or his crime. Most visits they talk about sports, cars, music. But Henry's waiting for the sermon. Sure enough, one day the chaplain looks Henry in the eye and says, "Henry, whatever you've done doesn't change who you *are*. You belong to the Creator, and you will always get my respect for that." Henry scoffed and changed the subject. But he had to admit, it felt good to hear. And after a while he opened up a bit. He and the chaplain got to talking about the stuff in Henry's life that was out of whack and about how things could get better.

You get the idea. There is great freedom when we don't need to prop up our *self* with fame and money and power or raise our relative worth by putting others down.

I should clarify that "grace" is not the same as "mercy." Grace relates to our *being*—who we are *intrinsically*. Grace is an antidote to the negative emotion of *shame*. Mercy applies to our *behavior* and has to do with releasing/being released from punishment or guilt.

Here's an example from my work life of how grace and mercy relate: As a professor, I tried to treat all of my students with the respect that their God-graced status gives them. I wanted the *best* for them. Sometimes that meant showing them mercy—overlooking an infraction or forgiving an assignment because they were overwhelmed by some crisis in their lives. But other times it meant imposing heavy discipline to help them bear down and get past a block in their studies. However, at all times I tried to see them through the eyes of *grace*: because we are all valuable to God, I would try to do whatever is *best* for *them*, for *myself*, and for the *relationship*. Depending on the situation, that could mean gentle listening, painful discipline, clear feedback, firm boundary setting, kind encouragement, or patient tutoring.

Jesus's Resurrection Gives Us an *Embodied* Hope

Christian scholars have spilled much ink arguing over the historicity of Jesus's resurrection. I happen to think that—as much as we can establish any particular event in the ancient past—there's pretty good evidence for it. But the *historicity* of Jesus's resurrection isn't the real point. As I've said, taking religion seriously means treating it like a computer app—*as if* it is real. The *power* in the story of Jesus's resurrection is that taking it seriously changes the way we treat our bodies and the land by giving us a different kind of *hope.*

Christian hope is often assumed to have something to do with a person's "soul" (conscious essence?) escaping from the body at death into a blessed realm that is outside of normal time and space. But there is actually very little in the Bible about that sort of thing. Christian scriptures focus instead on resurrection of the *body.*

Sadly, Christian hope has been contaminated for centuries by what scholars call "Gnosticism." Gnosticism was a Jewish-Christian movement in the second century CE that regarded the material world as a kind of prison for the "divine spark" (the soul) within us. Our bodies, the earth, all that we can physically sense was thought to be the creation not of God but of a "demiurge"—a lesser power who trapped our souls in "dirty" flesh. The key to freeing the soul was thought to be *enlightenment* (gnosis). However, the easy route to freedom was *death.* At death, Gnostics thought, the divine soul is liberated from its corrupt body and flies up to the "pleroma" (we call it "heaven" now)—a place of light inhabited by God and the angels.

Not only is gnostic hope body-denying, it also strips hope of its ability to fuel real-world *change*. For the most part, afterlife images (in many religious traditions, not just Jewish-Christian Gnosticism) are *static*. The believer is "asleep in the arms of Jesus," "reclining in a garden attended by bashful virgins and immortal youths," "dissolved into the universe," and so on. Such hopes reflect the desperate need for *rest and recovery* that we often feel in the midst of life's stress and deprivation. But rest is a *pause* in life, not a permanent state. It is meant to *renew* us for the challenges of our dynamic world, not to be an eternal condition. (As many unprepared retirees can tell you, *unending* rest can be excruciatingly boring!)

The earliest Christians pinned their hopes not on body-denial or eternal passivity but on the story of Jesus's physical transformation. They recognized the power it had to sustain healthy communities *now*.

Here's why. If all we can ultimately look forward to is *escape* from our body, then our body is just an unwanted husk, a rotting container that keeps us from our eternal destiny. We might even *long* to die (and in fact many do, or at least live as if they do!). It becomes easy to treat our bodies, others' bodies, the body of this Earth and its creatures, as disposable garbage. Enslavement, sexual assault, the rape of the earth, the ravages of war, alcoholism, gluttony, suicide, even genocide don't ultimately matter if bodies are just destined for the dump.

Jesus's resurrection, however, points toward a different kind of hope—the transformation of all things. It's not impossible. Scientists have already shown us the long history of transformation that our universe has been through—from darkness to light, energy to matter, matter to life, life to conscious, self-conscious, even God-conscious beings. Why should there not be another stage of that evolution ahead? That's how Paul speaks of the risen Jesus—as the "first fruit" (initial harvest) of a new humanity (1

Cor 15:20). In Christ, he also says, we are a "new creation" (2 Cor 5:17).

To believe in Jesus's resurrection is to believe that that evolution will take place *through* the struggles of this material world, not by escaping *from* them. Jesus's resurrected body bears the *scars* of his crucifixion. Those scars signal to us that his old body has been *changed*, but it has not been discarded. So, the new creation is not a *replacement* of the old, but a *transformation*. What we do to ourselves, other species, and the land now is *not* irrelevant in the long term. Because even as it evolves, the earth will bear into the future the scars of the crucifixions we inflict on it. Let's then treat ourselves and the land gently.

The resurrection of Jesus also helps prevent religion from being used as a narcotic. Philosopher Karl Marx once referred to religion as "the opiate of the masses." He was right. Otherworldly religion focused on the afterlife can function for communities like a painkiller does for people with terminal cancer: it allows them to live in peace while being consumed by an evil within. Oppressed people have often been pacified by the promise of a better deal in the life to come.

Historically, the nature of this analgesic effect has depended on the kind of deal that gnostic religion has made with its governing empire. Either the empire controls the outward structures of religion (e.g., state churches), leaving religion to look after the well-being of souls. Or religion and empire agree to divide the world into two sealed spheres—one run by the government and the market on "secular" principles of unfettered greed and political power, and the other (the personal interior life of the soul) on religious principles. And never the twain should meet.

This latter relationship is the current arrangement in Canada, and it may be the most odious. In Canada, registered charities can lose their tax-exempt status if they criticize government policies (no matter how unjust). But in return, religious groups are legally allowed to violate basic human rights—rights guaranteed for all Canadians in our Charter of Rights and Freedoms—just because they say, "We believe that a deity told us to do it this way."

So, for example, while it is illegal in Canada to "refuse to employ an individual . . . on a prohibited ground of discrimination"—which includes gender[1]—in many religious traditions women are still *prohibited by church law* from being hired as clergy! And the government allows it. In both Canada and the United States, a sample of groups (as of 2019) that *do not* allow ordination of women would include Roman Catholics, Southern Baptists, the Orthodox, Muslims, Missouri Synod Lutherans, Mormons, and Jewish Orthodox, among others. Even those groups that do ordain women often have trouble placing them in congregations, and only a handful have had a woman in the top leadership position. Similar forms of prohibited discrimination are practiced in some religious communities on the basis of sexual orientation, marital status, race, disability, and so on.

For me, Jesus's resurrection cancels the corrupt contract between gnostic religion and empire that tries to make faith irrelevant to our life as citizens. The one who was executed by *both* religious and political authorities because he challenged the death-dealing structures of his day was raised by God from the grave. That seems like a pretty clear sign from God that empire and religion got it wrong.

Churches have often tried to conceal this mess by interpreting Jesus's ministry as a metaphor for the life of the soul. So, in the Lord's Prayer, "forgiving our debtors" (i.e., those who owe us *money*) became "forgiving the *guilt* of people who offend us." The "kingdom of heaven" (better translated "reign of God") became a kind of parallel spiritual universe somewhere beyond this world. Jesus's angry protest in the temple, when he overthrew the tables of the money-changers who were robbing the poor, became a sign that religion should have nothing to do with economics.

I have to concede that, at the other extreme, Jesus has also been used as a symbol for radical violence. His passionate defense of the poor and stinging critiques of the powerful have been taken as license to bomb and burn in the name of revolution. But there is no evidence from Jesus's ministry that he would have condoned the terrorism that replaces one form of oppression with another.

Even so, the sheer physicality of the resurrection stories does remind us that faith is meant to be *embodied*, that faith is an energy that drives us toward the *healing* of God's broken world, not *escape* from it. And Jesus's resurrection calls us to open ourselves to a God who is not hiding in a heaven far off but gazing at us through the eyes of our neighbor and working through both of us to give this suffering planet a better future.

Explore!

1. Look back to the Explore! section at the end of chapter 2, and remember what you said made you feel won-der-*full*. Now imagine that thing was removed from your life altogether. What would change?

2. Imagine a ten-year-old child (perhaps your own) coming to you and asking, "I learned that there are different religions in school today. What do you believe? Why?" What key things would you say to her, in a way that she could understand? Discuss it with a family member?

3. Discuss with a conversation partner: Which part of Cam Harder's faith story do you connect best with and why? Which element seems most foreign to you and why?

4. Read the conclusion (immediately after this chapter—it's only a couple of pages). How does the image of God as "weaver" impact you?

5. Write down two things that you want to take away from the experience of reading and discussing this book. How will you incorporate those two things into your view of the world or your involvement with a religious organization? Consider sharing a bit of that with friends on social media.

Notes

1. *Canadian Human Rights Act*, 1985, Part 1:7, "Employment," accessed September 20, 2019, https://tinyurl.com/ygs5adgt.

Decision Time: Is There Room for Religion in the Twenty-First Century?

I don't often read nonfiction books in order, from page one to the end. Usually I zoom in first on the chapters that interest me most, then cast around for more detail. Sometimes I start at the end so I know where the author is heading and can plan my own journey.

If you have worked through the book, exploring along the way, you will have reached your own conclusions about whether there is room for faith and religion in the twenty-first century.

If you're starting at the end to see where I'm going, then here's my conclusion. Yes, I am convinced that there is not only room, but a real need for, healthy religion in the future that our children will inherit. More than ever, when climate change and habitat loss are threatening life on our planet in ways unprecedented in human memory, they will need social structures that allow them to move beyond survival mode—to grieve, hope, and work *together*.

And if you personally can use some of what I have written to help you find, or refine, a religious tradition that is life-affirming, I will feel that this effort has been worthwhile.

With her permission, I will leave you with an image of God from poet and theologian Marchiene Rienstra that has touched me. It's not conventional (and that's good!). It pulls together many of the threads we've explored in this book.

To Weavers Everywhere[1]

God sits weeping,
    The beautiful creation tapestry
    She wove with such joy
    is mutilated, torn into shreds,
    reduced to rags
    its beauty fragmented by force.
God sits weeping.
    But look!
    She is gathering up the shreds
    to weave something new.
She gathers
    our shreds of sorrow—
    the pain, the tears, the frustration
    caused by cruelty, crushing
    ignoring, violating, killing.
She gathers
    the rags of hard work
    attempts at advocacy
    initiatives for peace
    protests against injustice
    all the seemingly little and weak
    words and deeds offered
    sacrificially
    in hope, in faith, in love.
And look!
She is weaving them all
    with golden threads of Jubilation
    into a new tapestry,
    a creation richer, more beautiful
    than the old one was!

God sits weaving
   patiently, persistently
   with a smile that
   radiates like a rainbow
   on her tear-streaked face.
And She invites us
   not only to keep offering her the
   shreds and rags of our suffering
   and our work
But even more—
   to take our place beside Her
   at the Jubilee Loom
   and weave with Her
   the Tapestry of the New Creation.

—Marchiene Rienstra

Notes

1. Marchiene Rienstra, "To Weavers Everywhere," in *Take Up the Song* (Toronto: Ten Days, 1996), 4–5. Reproduced with the author's permission.

Explore Further

The endnotes for each chapter provide many opportunities for further exploration. This bibliography highlights some references that I have found particularly useful or comprehensive and adds a few more that might extend your conversation on the chapter topics.

Primary Sources

Engaging Tough Questions

Living the Questions. https://livingthequestions.com. This stimulating set of videos, podcasts, and print resources comes from a variety of scientists, theologians, and others. It might be uncomfortable for traditional congregations but has lots of great conversation starters for people considering the faith, or mature Christians who are rethinking it and for whom no questions are out of bounds. Their segment "Painting the Stars" is particularly evocative.

The Origins of Religion

Hoffman, Donald. "Do we see reality as it is?" *TED Talks.* Youtube.com. Accessed August 5, 2019, https://tinyurl.com/ngykz97. Hoffman's description of how our brain creates an artificial interface with reality was my inspiration for thinking of religions as "apps" or "God-user-interfaces."

Holloway, Richard. *A Little History of Religion.* New Haven: Yale University Press, 2016. Former head of the Anglican Church in Scotland, now a broadcaster and religious agnostic, Holloway explores the origins of religion with a sense of humor and open-minded skepticism.

Smith, Christian. *Religion: What It Is, How It Works, and Why It Matters.* Princeton: Princeton University Press, 2017. Somewhat more positive toward religion than Holloway's book.

Miracles and Mysterious Moments

Nagasawa, Yujin. *Miracles: A Very Short Introduction.* Oxford: Oxford University Press, 2018. Philosopher Nagasawa looks at the origins of belief in the miraculous, and its role in various religions, drawing on a variety of interesting mysteries and coincidences. He challenges the idea that miracles are useful in modern thinking.

Strobel, Lee. *The Case for Miracles: A Journalist Investigates Evidence for the Supernatural.* Grand Rapids: Zondervan, 2018. Journalist and former pastor Lee Strobel make a case against and for miracles. It is well written, but ultimately intended as a defense of the miraculous.

Religion and Violence

Armstrong, Karen. "Is religion the root of the world's conflicts?" Interview with Mehdi Hasan of Al Jazeera. Armstrong is a former Irish Catholic nun, now an author and teacher in comparative religion. She does an excellent job of teasing out the political, economic, and religious strands involved in terrorist violence, from the IRA to ISIS.

Brous, Sharon. "It's time to reclaim religion." TedWomen 2016. https://tinyurl.com/yzpcza5t. Delivers a stirring talk calling people of faith to move out of their "religious routine-ism" to deal with twenty-first-century challenges of violence and prejudice. A couple of good stories and some great illustrations.

Yaqeen Institute for Islamic Research. "Is Islam a Religion of Violence?" https://tinyurl.com/yf7k8rdr. An accessible animated video that very clearly distinguishes what Islam teaches (and the vast majority of Muslims believe) from what is often presented in the media about Islam and terrorism.

Religion and Child Sexual Abuse

Australian Royal Commission into Institutional Responses to Child Sexual Abuse (ARC). *Final Report*, 2017. https://tinyurl.com/yjlms7jy. This is a massive multivolume study of child sexual abuse in Australia. It is available online, well indexed, and full of direct quotes from survivors. It is perhaps the most complete resource available from any country on this topic and is quite readable and searchable.

Canadian Baptists of Western Canada. *Preventing Abuse in the Church: Abuse Prevention Policies and Recommendations.* Calgary, AB, 2017. https://tinyurl.com/yeh7c9ec. This is an excellent example of a religious community's policy for protection of children and other vulnerable people. Has concrete list of things to "watch for" to make early intervention possible.

Doyle, Thomas P. "Abbreviated Bibliography of Selected Sources Related to Clergy Sexual Abuse, Ecclesiastical Politics, Theology and Church History," *Voice of the Faithful*, revised August 12, 2013. Accessed November 19, 2018, https://tinyurl.com/ydvfezl5. Particularly points to sources related to the Catholic sphere. The endnotes for chapter 4 contain references for religious and nonreligious contexts other than Catholic.

Plante, Thomas. "Four Lessons Learned from Treating Catholic Priest Sex Offenders." *Pastoral Psychology* 64, no. 3 (June 2015), 407–12. https://scholarcommons.scu.edu/psych/75/. Plante has been working with Catholic Priest sex offenders for many years. It is perhaps more sympathetic to offenders than some may be comfortable with, but is nuanced and insightful.

Starks, Glen L. *Sexual Misconduct and the Future of Large Mega-Churches: How Large Religious Organizations Go Astray*. Santa Barbara, CA: ABC-CLIO, 2013. Deals with sexual abuse, including children, especially in evangelical churches—an area that hasn't had much media attention.

The Benefits of Religion to Society

Ammerman, Nancy. *Congregation and Community*. New Brunswick, NJ: Rutgers University Press, 1996. This book, along with *Congregations in Transition*, which Ammerman wrote with Carl Dudley, provides a wonderful set of stories and tools to help faith communities connect more vitally and positively with their communities.

Gunderson, Gary. *Deeply Woven Roots: Improving the Quality of Life in Your Community.* Minneapolis: Fortress Press, 1997. This book has been very helpful for me in understanding some of the unique gifts that faith groups bring to their communities.

Harder, Cameron. *Discovering the Other: Asset-based Approaches for Building Community Together.* Lanham, MD: Rowman & Littlefield, 2013. Asset-based strategies for re-invigorating depressed, depleted communities and organizations are becoming more common. This is my effort to provide a trinitarian Christian framework for such strategies and to provide some tools that a variety of religious leaders can use—with appropriate interpretation—in their faith communities.

Science and Faith

Alan Wallace, *Contemplative Science: Where Buddhism and Neuroscience Converge* (New York: Columbia University Press, 2007). Creative connections between meditation, Buddhist philosophy, and brain science.

Bekoff, Mark, and Jessica Pierce. *Wild Justice: The Moral Life of Animals.* Chicago: University of Chicago Press, 2010. Demonstrates continuity between humans and animals with examples of how animals practice altruism, fairness, and other ethical virtues. For shorter pieces, more focused on animal *emotion and consciousness*, see Barbara King, "The Orca's Sorrow," *Scientific American* 320, no. 3 (March 2019): 30–35 and Daniel Zuckerbrot, "Mysteries of the Animal Mind," CBC's *The Nature of Things*, May 16, 2015, https://tinyurl.com/yk23rga7 (latter only available in Canada).

Nidhal Guessoum. *The Young Muslim's Guide to Modern Science.* Manchester, UK: Beacon Books, 2017. A Muslim scientist's effort to help parents and children in religious homes to engage scientific questions with open-minded curiosity. Great for all ages.

Polkinghorne, John. *Quarks, Chaos & Christianity: Questions to Science and Religion.* 2nd edition. New York: Crossroad, 2005. Renowned physicist and Anglican priest, Polkinghorne is perhaps the best-known twentieth-century Christian writer in the science and religion area. Especially helpful in understanding how dependent science is on "stories" (theories).

Suffering

Dalai Lama, Desmond Tutu, and Douglas Carlton Abrams. *The Book of Joy: Lasting Happiness in a Changing World.* New York: Viking, 2016. Wonderful book written by two old friends—Buddhist leader the Dalai Lama, and Christian leader Bishop Desmond Tutu, who have both suffered a great deal. With the help of journalist Douglas Abrams, they describe how to find peace and joy in the midst of suffering. Very readable and insightful.

Hall, Douglas John. *God and Human Suffering: An Exercise in the Theology of the Cross.* Minneapolis: Fortress Press, 1986. Douglas John Hall is perhaps the most well-known Canadian theologian of the twentieth century. This classic sets out and compares the most common approaches to understanding suffering within a religious context.

Yancey, Philip. "Where Is God When It Hurts?" in *What Good Is God? In Search of a Faith That Matters.* Nashville, TN: Faith Words, 2010, pp. 25–35. This is Yancey's address in the chapel at

Virginia Tech just after the shooting of thirty-two people. Honest and compassionate.

Why I Am a Christian

Hordern, William. *Living by Grace.* Philadelphia: Westminster, 1975. My seminary professor and a well-known Canadian-American theologian. This is a classic work that has strongly influenced my personal faith and theology.

Additional Resources in Areas Touched On in the Book

Religion and Ecology

Interfaith Power and Light. *Religious Statements on Climate Change.* https://tinyurl.com/yftkbj6h. Great place to access statements on climate change from a variety of religions. A selection of religious texts that speak to environmental protection from various traditions can also be found on the UN site at https://tinyurl.com/yfblv6q7.

Lutherans Restoring Creation. https://lutheransrestoringcreation.org/. In spite of the rather presumptive name, this is a good selection of activities, stories, and other resources to help leaders green their congregations. Many can be adapted to non–Christian settings.

Foley, Jonathan. "Can We Feed the World, Sustain the Planet?" *Scientific American* 305, no. 5 (2011), 60–65. This is a meta-study (study of many studies) looking at the key sources of greenhouse gases. You may be surprised by the findings. Well presented.

Religion and Indigenous Peoples

Truth and Reconciliation Commission of Canada. https://tinyurl.com/ye2efdcf. This web address takes you to the final report of the Canadian commission that investigated Indian Residential Schools. The website is also a portal to other resources on this horrifying history.

Treat, James, ed. *Native and Christian: Indigenous Voices on Religious Identity in the United States and Canada*. New York: Routledge, 1996. "Theology" as a set of universal beliefs is not normal to Indigenous religion, which tends to value personal and tribal experience. This difference from European religion may have contributed to colonial dismissal of indigenous spirituality. This book is a series of articles that tries to bridge the two.

Statistics on Religion: Canada and the United States

Pew Research Center. https://www.pewresearch.org/. A treasure house of careful research on religion and science, politics, economics and other matters. Primarily American research but Canadian and global too.

Public Religion Research Institute. Https://www.prri.org. Along with the Pew Research Centre, this group provides reliable, clearly presented data on various topics related to religion in America in its "Religion and Culture" section.

Bibby, Reginald. *Resilient Gods*. Vancouver, UBC Press, 2017. Bibby is Canada's most well-known sociologist of religion. This and his many other books over several decades paint a vivid picture of the changing landscape of religion in Canada. You can see them all at http://www.reginaldbibby.com/booksmonographs.html.

Statistics Canada. https://www.statcan.gc.ca. Provides info from Canadian census—including religion, charitable giving, and other population data.